ASTROLOGY FOR DOGS

D1518787

BY
LINDA L. LACY

ASTROLOGY FOR DOGS

how to understand,

train and love your dog

with sun signs and moon signs

BY
LINDA L. LACY

Illustrator **Chris Bagdenoff**

DENLINGER'S PUBLISHERS, LTD.
Box 76, Fairfax, Virginia 22030

Library of Congress Cataloging-in-Publication Data

Lacy, Linda,
    Astrology for dogs : how to understand, train, and
love your dog with sun signs and moon signs / by Linda
Lacy.
      p. cm.
    ISBN 0-87714-142-8
    1. Astrology and pets. 2. Dogs — Miscellanes. I.
Title.
BF1728.3.L33 1990   89-29516
133.5 ′86367—dc20

                         CIP

International Standard Book Number : 0-87714-142-8

Dedicated to
my Libra companion L.L.T.

ACKNOWLEDGEMENTS

I am grateful to E.T. Farris for her help and encouragement in using astrology with pets, and to E.V.H. for his understanding.

My appreciation also to Dr. Reghetti, veterinarian, for his review of the manuscript.

I am also grateful to all the dog lovers I met during the writing of this book who were willing to share their pet stories and sun signs.

A special thanks to my dog friends Curly, Peaches, Lucky, Walla, Darcy, Benji, and especially Lancy, who not only brightened my life, but also, taught me about living.

Table of Contents

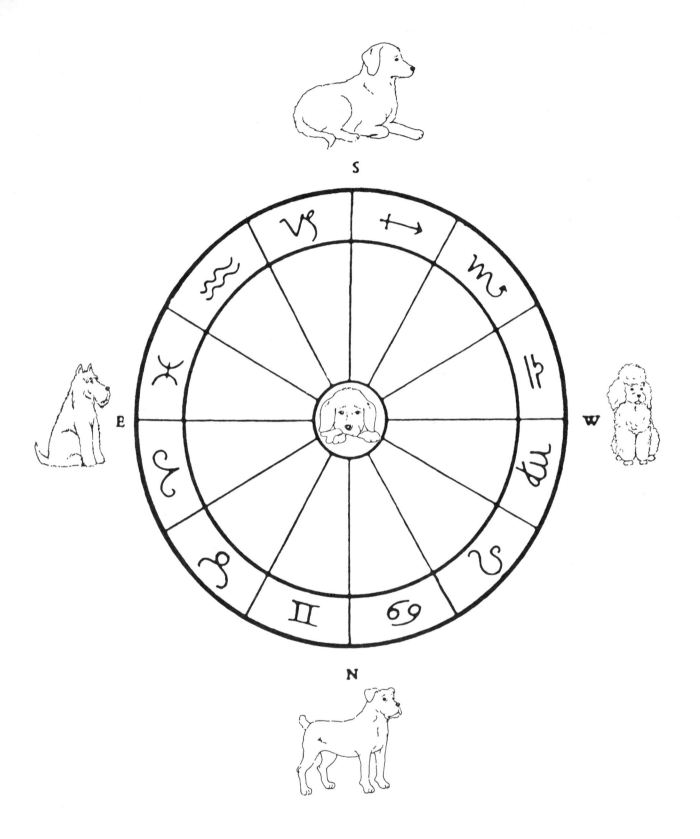

Preface

SUN SIGNS, the first section of this book, will give you some insight to the following three categories:

The Puppy—Making your new friend feel at home, and surviving the adjustment yourself.

Training—Hints on education with astrology, and help in your own leadership role.

Public Relations—The social climate your dog enjoys, and how you can become better adjusted to each other.

MOON SIGNS, the second section, will provide a short sketch of your pet's character. Be sure to read the introduction to Moon signs carefully, since Moon signs may be more difficult to identify than Sun signs.

The Moon sign governs the type of impression your pooch will make on his or her public. If the Moon has a strong influence, your pet will tend to be well-behaved, peaceful, gentle, and mild-mannered. A dominant Moon will also cause a pet to be restless.

The Moon is an important sign for pets because it rules the senses—taste, touch, hearing, sight, and smell— and how the dog relates to the physical world.

The **Moon Signs** section will include the following three categories:

Emotional Nature—How the Moon influences your pet's emotional temperament.

The World of the Moon Sign—A look at how your dog sees, and adjusts to his environment.

Personal Relationships—Getting along with your own Moon sign pet.

Another important feature of your pet's makeup is the ascendant—the sign of First House determined by the month, day, and time of your pet's birth. The ascendant travels through all the signs in one day and will result in litter-mates having different ascendants, and different natures.

THE CONCLUSION illustrates some possible combinations of Sun and Moon signs. There are some hints on how to look at these combinations in relation to your dog's individual makeup.

The artist's drawings for each chapter in this book are not meant to depict any specific breed. The dogs illustrated represent a composite of the attributes of each Zodiac sign.

Please be sure to use this book as a means to understand and love your dog. Any questions about health, nutrition, grooming, or disease should be referred to your local veterinarian.

Experience has shown me that you can develop a better understanding of anyone—including dogs or other creatures in the home—through an emphatic knowledge of astrology. Hopefully, this book will give you an astrological insight into the temperament of your pet.

This book was written to assist you, the reader, to live more happily with your pet.

According to today's popular view of astrology, the Sun sign is given great significance. The Sun sign is an influential feature because it is the center of our planetary system. It is also easy to work with because it is in approximately the same position each year on any given day. The other planets do not move as regularly, and can be in different signs in different years on a given day.

The Sun Signs

Sun Signs

A Sun sign refers to the sign of the Zodiac the Sun was in on the day or night your puppy was born. It is usually easy to find the Sun sign for your pet by checking his or her registration papers for the date of birth.

If your pet does not have papers, you may be able to remember that special day you brought your new friend home. It may be possible to call his or her breeder or "first home" and count back the appropriate number of weeks to the birthday. When you arrive at a definite birthday, check the dates listed for each Sign until you find your pet.

If your dog is "a child of the universe," the birthday will be your own estimate. Try to narrow down the birthdate to two or three months and you will probably be able to identify a sign that matches your dog.
In a case where you have acquired a "mature stranger," a review of all the signs may shed some light on the appropriate sign at birth.

When you find the day of birth, problems may arise if your dog was born on the cusp, which means at the beginning or end of a Sun sign. If your dog was born on the first or last day of a Sun sign, you may need to know the hour of birth and the location to check when the Sun changed signs. (The Sun may change signs in the morning, afternoon, or evening of a day.) If in doubt of the exact date, you can read both Sun signs, and then make an intuitive guess.

At the beginning of each Sun sign you will see four categories: element, symbol, polarity, and ruling planet.

Element refers to the four elements of fire, earth, air, and water that are represented by the Zodiac signs.

Symbol refers to the constellation representing the nature of the Sun sign. For example: Aries is the Ram, Taurus the Bull.

Polarity refers to the yin or yang of each Sun sign. Some signs have a feminine bent and some have a masculine leaning. The polarity has nothing to do with the sex of the Sun sign or the sexuality of your pet.

Not wanting to be a sexist, I searched for another way of referring to your pet in place of he/she or it. The Zodiac solved my problem with the polarity signs. Therefore, with signs that represent the yang, or masculine bent, I refer to the dog as he, and the yin, or feminine, as she.

Ruling planet refers to the planet representing the nature of the sign: Mars—called the planet of war—represents the aggressive nature of Aries, and Venus—the planet of love—represents the affectionate nature of Taurus.

If the description of a Sun sign does not match your pet, remember that there are many astrological influences involved, including: Moon signs (see Part II), ascendants (the First House determined by the month, day, and time of birth), and the position of the planets in the Twelve Houses.

Only a complete natal chart based upon the exact day, time, and location of your pet's birth will give you an in-depth understanding of your dog. In lieu of this, knowing his or her Sun sign and perhaps Moon sign will help you understand your dog's nature and needs.

Most dog lovers will agree that their pets often exhibit characteristics that are unusual for the pet's breed, heredity, or environment. A look at the Sun sign may fill in the missing influences.

It may enable you to be more patient with your picky Virgo, and less annoyed by bossy Aries.

So, on to the Sun signs.

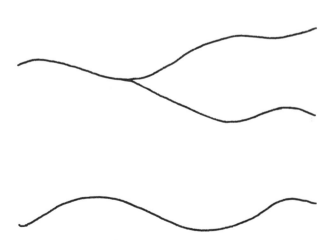

Aries

Aries

March 21-April 20
Element—Fire
Symbol—The Ram
Polarity—Yang, Masculine
Ruling Planet—Mars

The Puppy

Aries puppies are the pride of every breeder. They are definitely alert. The little rams are early to open their eyes, early to walk, and full of spirit.

You will recognize an Aries litter by their mother. She will be a little frantic and overwhelmed by a parcel of puppies who all want to be first. They will be playfully stepping on each other's ears to be first in the lunch line, climbing over each other to be first for a lick or a cuddle.

It will be hard to decide which puppy is yours because they all will be frisky and bubbly—great performers for attention and affection. All these puppies are born leaders and not too diplomatic about their desire and right to attention. Males and females both exhibit all the tendencies to perform and achieve, and neither sex knows what defeat means.

When you finally pick your squirming little ball of fire, he will go home with you as the conquering hero. Once in your home he will survey the situation: the physical surroundings and the "pecking order" (if there are other animals or children involved), and then he will rightfully assert his claim to authority. You think you have chosen him, but he has chosen you.

If your Aries is going to be a house pet, you need not worry about providing the standard new puppy paraphernalia of soft blankets and sheltered sleeping quarters. If confined, he will howl and devise enterprising methods of escaping large cartons or closed-off kitchens. Persistence is the word; no challenge of closed doors or pet boxes is too big for him. He will howl all night or chew through cardboard. If you give him his freedom (your nerves are shot anyway), he will happily investigate the area, and you may find him in the morning in an exhausted heap in your closet.

Aries pups are a handful, but they have redeeming qualities. His fiery disposition may appear to be irrational, or even stubborn at times, but he is intelligent and courageous.

Those little problems of digging under fences, climbing through or over fences, or just scaling them with one giant leap, are not because he is testing your patience. Fences are a challenge, restrictions are a challenge, leashes are a challenge. He loves his freedom.

An Aries puppy must be kept busy. He doesn't observe his world, he controls it, by chewing—indefinitely—and barking. He's very talkative.

An Aries puppy has a high energy level and must be exercised. This is for your own safety. He is an explorer and may start many investigations into his world. He may not finish all his projects—thank goodness for small holes in the yard that might have been bigger—but he needs to be free to start new tasks.

One Aries puppy, when left at home too long, completely stripped a king sized bed by pulling at one corner of each quilt, blanket, sheet, and pad and then running the length of the room. Bed clothes were stacked in separate but equal piles at the wall: boredom is a terrible thing for an Aries.

Another ambitious Aries discovered toilet paper rolls, and pulled varying lengths to all parts of the house. The returning owners thought the house had been vandalized.

The little Aries will need training, but he will smart under discipline if it is too harsh and may be driven to rebellion. The lucky Aries owner realizes the intelligence of his fiery pet and runs madly for the dog training manuals to assert authority.

Good luck. This may be tricky.

Training

You have all the basic ingredients with your diamond-in-the-rough. He is intelligent, self-confident, and determined. Training can begin early for the Aries puppy for two reasons: he is a ready, willing, and able explorer, and you will need all the help that a headstart can give.

Your Aries pup will be unaware he is causing any problem. He is rather naive in a way, yet fearless.

15

Probably the best way to begin training is by enrolling him in scheduled dog training. Again, there are two reasons. An Aries dog loves to be first. He will really excel competing with the rest of the students. He also loves the challenge of performing before an audience. And you may need professional assistance in your leadership role.

Remember, the Aries student loves praise, and he thrives on it. He may appear not to need it because of his self-confidence, but praise is his reason for excelling.

You will notice that he has a temper (the holes in your socks when you left him too long), but on the training field his temper can usually be kept in tow if the commands are challenging yet respectful. He is never angry for long. His temper may flare, but it extinguishes itself quickly.

Give commands in a pleasant, firm tone, and he'll think of them as requests.

Don't make your training sessions boring; he loves variety. Whatever you try to teach him, he will give his all. He will try over and over again to please. Nothing can break his spirit.

He may be impatient, that fiery willfulness, but much of this is due to an over-supply of energy. A good long run before training can do wonders. He will still be alert, but not ready to burst at the seams. You, on the other hand may be ready for a nap.

Although an Aries pooch needs and benefits from good training and discipline, don't be harsh. An occasional Aries may turn quite nasty if handled roughly and without frequent rewards.

He may often be in a hurry, so careful observation of the training of the "heel" technique is a must. He may have a tendency to try to walk you, instead of walking with you.

He will be a quick learner but impulsive and pugnacious. His rapid grasp of the essentials may cause him to overlook details. For example: The Collie who quickly responded to a sit command, and ignored the fact that he had promptly sat on a Miniature Poodle. He is not a diplomat.

During the basic training class you and your dog can become a great team. You will learn a lot about him and yourself. He will be ready and eager to take advanced training and the higher variety of obedience work. If you are an Aries, perhaps you will too.

Public Relations

A dog who is boss may seem hard to live with, but don't let his leadership and self-confidence fool you. Aries can't stand to appear weak or dependent. He is very sensitive, but he would rather die than admit it.

The ram will be very direct and honest with very little tact or humility. He is one of the few Sun signs, with the exception of Scorpio, that can look someone straight in the eye for hours. You may be the one that blinks first.

Your Arian loves anything new and is quickly bored. He is impatient, so don't leave him waiting in your car too long. If things get dull he may chew the seat belts or explore the glove compartment.

Despite all his bravery and confidence, he hates pain. The Aries dog is a sissy about physical hurts. His independence fades at the veterinarian's as he awaits his rabies shot. If injured, he will whimper and carry on much longer than dogs of other Sun signs. Lots of love and care will make you a real hero to him at this time.

Aries has amazing recuperative powers after an illness or injury. He heals quickly, if you confine him so that he will allow himself to rest before going on to his next challenge.

Aries is fiercely loyal, and if he knows you are his master, you can do no wrong. He will not be domestic like a home-loving Libra; his adventurous spirit loves freedom.

Aries is aggressive and impetuous. His bravery will impress, if not shock, you.

On a more intimate level, your Arian needs to express his sexuality more than most signs. The Aries male needs the time and freedom to "strut his stuff." He'll be deeply frustrated if he's not allowed to mark off his territory and sniff at all the female dogs. The Aries female requires freedom and variety as well. She will be loyal to you, but she'll demand novelty and variety in her social life.

The Aries is a finicky eater. He will try anything once—the need to explore. But, if he doesn't like it, don't bother putting it in his dish. Most Aries can use extra potassium phosphate in their meals for extra energy. Few dogs will gobble up a raw tomato (an excellent source of potassium phosphate), but they may enjoy spaghetti sauce over their dog chow.

Aries dogs do make wonderful partners once you are aware of their basic drives. Aries is self-conscious, but not vain. He will react to how you see his behavior. Part of his partnership ability comes from the fact that he is a people watcher.

Be sure to consider the breed of your Aries friend, as breeds enhance specific qualities at times that may or may not match the model Aries. Consequently, you may find an exaggerated Aries in a Doberman guard dog, or an insecure leader blooming under a delicate Cocker Spaniel. Moon signs (see the Preface) should be consulted, if possible, as they influence the emotional nature.

Whatever the Moon sign, the Aries dog will take some form of leadership role. It could be leading you or the neighborhood pets. Just remember, you are living with the boss.

Notes on Your Aries Dog

The Puppy _____
_____
_____
_____
_____
_____

Training _____
_____
_____
_____
_____
_____

Public Relations _____
_____
_____
_____
_____
_____

Taurus

Taurus

April 21-May 21
Element — Earth
Symbol — The Bull
Polarity — Yin, Feminine
Ruling Planet — Venus

The Puppy

Your Taurus pup will be calm, passive, and affectionate, especially if she gets her own way. Taurus litters are a joy to any new mother. They love the security of home and family. They are rather slow-moving, even as pups, and there will be no mad dashes to the lunch line as with Aries.

Taurus will be charming and easily led as tiny puppies. Once they are old enough to come home, be on your toes.

Your new puppy dislikes change and worships her home, so she may be more upset than other signs about any alterations in her living arrangements.

Your pup may ask "Where's Mom and the gang?" She'll need lots of love and gentle attention to adjust to your home. Taurus is not a very adaptable sign, as you will soon see.

Little Taurus is very sensual and will love a soft place to sleep. She will also tend to over-eat to the point of illness, so watch her food allotment.

One Taurus youngster joined a home-made ice cream party. She was so sweet everyone fed her. At the end of the evening she was found unconscious on the kitchen floor, her little belly about to burst. Taurus will eat until there is no more room and then eat more.

You will find your little bull to be quite head-strong despite her calm, loving exterior. She will not be rushed, and she doesn't like to take risks. She will survey every situation in her patient, plodding way before she considers action. Unlike Sagittarius, she will not dash off after lizards or butterflies. She's a conservative, and if her Moon sign does not counteract her need for slow deliberation, she may be a bit boring.

Taurus has a tendency to be very possessive. This trait should be disciplined in puppyhood to prevent your Taurus from taking over your home. She will need some things that are strictly her own, such as, her dish, bed, and leash, but let her know some things must be shared. If there are other pets or children in the home, little Taurus should be trained to share toys. When she is a tiny pup, practice taking her chew chew or toy bone. If she growls, a firm reprimand is in order. What she learns as a puppy will be remembered, and save you embarrassment and doctor bills when she's older.

Your little bull has a great love of permanence, and as a pup you will see she enjoys rules and a set routine. She is a plodder, so don't force her too young or too soon. She will make slow progress, but everything she learns will be retained forever. She'll be a warm, affectionate teenager. Sure and determined, her style will impress you even if she doesn't have the originality of the Sagittarius.

Taurus pups have the early maturity of Capricorn and Scorpio, but don't let this fool you. She is not to be forced, and can be quite bull-headed if she feels pushed. Your little bull will respond to lots of hugs and petting. Her quiet sweetness is a plus, again when she gets her own way. Lots of loving will melt her stubbornness, and she'll be her practical, reliable self again.

The Taurus puppy may be a little sloppy—dripping water and food around her dish—and she will often get dirty in the yard. She will also have a good sense of smell, and may persist in following her nose to places she is not needed.

She can be a little tough on furniture despite her great love of home. She loves the snug, cozy atmosphere of indoors, but may need to be reminded to stay off the sofa.

Your affection will melt her occasional obstinate behavior and inflexibility. Loving praise will be a must in her training.

Training

The bull has a calm, determined attitude about training. She's strong-willed and self-indulgent at times. Remember, Taurus is slow-moving and slow-thinking. Be patient. If she feels pressed she'll become resentful and obstinate. Her slow endurance has its benefits.

Taurus will not scatter her attention or be distracted by other dogs. What she learns in her methodical way will be retained. She's trustworthy too, and logical in her approach to learning.

She'll work best in carefully planned training. Get a good book or attend training classes. She will be unduly upset by even tiny deviations from the normal training routine. Try to train at the same hour daily and for equal time periods. Give commands in the same way, using the same word, tone, and manner. She'll be a stickler for precise routine, and her responses will be solid, steady, and reliable. She might just be the star of her class if she can overcome her uncompromising fear of change.

The typical Taurus hates orders but loves affection. Be forewarned. Yelling and harsh voices will close her ears. She will quit and be resentful of your lack of diplomacy. Taurus is also belligerent if teased or forced to do what she does not want to do. When coerced, she will be silent and moody. You wondered why her symbol was the bull?

To handle defiance, turn on the affection. Scratching behind the ears will open them to reason again. If your commands are practical and honest, she will obey. Nothing complicated please. Your Taurus has good, common sense. She's industrious and loves to learn in a methodical way. She'll do well on tests, as she is not flighty or impressed by the tension in the class.

Your Taurus will mind her own business in school. She doesn't like to perform in public as the main attraction. Her public will know she doesn't need or want their advice in training. Your love and encouragement will be enough.

Public Relations

As a parent, Taurus is very possessive. Don't pick up her pups unless you have her permission. Don't remove the pups from her sight unless you are prepared for Mom's hysteria.

Taurus males make good guards. They watch over their possessions constantly, probably including you and your family.

Remember the early training about sharing her toys? Depending on her Moon sign and her breed, you may need to encourage her to share you. She may be cordial to your friends if she trusts them, but don't expect her to be the diplomat.

You will need to encourage your bull to try new things. She has a tendency to get in a rut and refuse to change routines or attitudes. She loves permanence and stands like a rock amidst any storm of change.

Taurus is very slow to be aroused, but when finally angry can be a terror. You may never have to endure this anger, but warn your friends not to push her too far.

The Taurus dog prefers the country to the city, but if born in the city she will resist the move to the country even if she loves the fresh air and grass. She just hates change.

One Taurus gal was really upset by her family's move to a neighborhood of new tract homes. She balked at going in the new house and sulked off down the street. In the rush of unpacking, the owners didn't miss her until evening. After a short search they found her sitting at the door-step to an empty, identical house down the street. She was lost, disoriented, and not at all happy with her new surroundings.

Taurus also loves soft music and luxury. Her main luxury is food. She loves to eat, although she can be picky about food. Her likes and dislikes are formed early and definitely, so give her a variety of dishes when a pup. When she's grown up it may be too late to add something new to her menu.

Taurus normally has good health, but if ill she recuperates slowly. She does everything slowly. She may be sensitive to problems with the throat or neck. Sore throats can be a problem. The Taurus tends toward large bodies and full necks, again depending on the breed. They may have weight problems or poor circulation in later years. Taurus needs fresh air and exercise, or she may become lethargic.

Taurus is not easily ruffled or disturbed, and her normally calm, pleasant manner is a blessing. She'll always think she is being patient, not stubborn or shy.

She is never nervous or twitchy. She'll be the stoic, strong, silent type even if you feel she is obstinate.

If you need a predictable home-body, Taurus is your girl. You will be great friends, especially if your own signs show a love of home and a need for routine.

Notes on Your Taurus Dog

The Puppy

_____
_____
_____
_____
_____
_____

Training

_____
_____
_____
_____
_____
_____

Public Relations

_____
_____
_____
_____
_____

Gemini

Gemini

May 22-June 21
Element — Air
Symbol — The Twins
Polarity — Yang, Masculine
Ruling Planet — Mercury

The Puppy

A Gemini litter looks like a beehive of activity. They are dashing back and forth and seem to be two places at once. If your Sun sign is the twins, you can be two places at one time.

Gemini puppies will slip out of your grasp and be off scurrying from one person to another. They love to communicate and will wiggle so hard you know they have something to say.

Once installed in your home, your Gemini's need to communicate will be more pronounced. He will love to address others, and even as a pup may become the spokesman of the neighborhood. This may include being a little too yappy. If left alone, he may begin long conversations with neighborhood dogs. Fences or doors won't hinder him. He is born to gossip.

Your Gemini pup is easily bored. He'll need lots of toys and distractions to keep him from talking or whining to himself. Gemini tends to be restless, inquisitive, and lives on nervous energy. It's amazing what a little guy can do in one afternoon on his own. He can investigate everything in his back yard, including uprooting plants and digging up sprinkler systems.

Your pup hates to be confined in small places. He needs to seek, explore and learn. If he is cooped up too much he may suffer from emotional depression, or your neighbors may complain about his verbose nature. His nervous energy can result in continuous barking.

A Gemini is fidgety. This is the hyperactive sign of the zodiac. His fiery mind and quick movements make him a little jumping jack.

Let him get used to wearing a collar early. He won't be wild about any form of restraint. He may slip his collar—just to get a better look at it, of course. Introduce him to a leash at a young age as well. His lively romping may make it necessary for you to try a harness instead of a collar. Although he can't slip his harness as he can the collar, he won't like the harness any better. Try to explain that it is necessary for his own safety on the street, and then take him for a walk where there are lots of other dogs. He will have to stop and converse at any residence with pets and people at home. He is very friendly and his need to communicate will practically turn him inside out.

A Gemini needs something new each day. If his mind isn't kept busy he may get sneaky and seek new thrills on his own.

He is tense, quick-moving and wiry. He'll love light sports but nothing too rough.

Most Gemini dogs love to travel and are excellent riders. Cars will be a Gemini's vehicle to adventure and new places to stop and chat.

All that restless energy may be a little hard to take. He loves to start new things and seems to skim the surfaces of life. He won't like discipline, but needs to be encouraged to finish what he starts. A Gemini will need help with self-control, especially if he is going to go on to formal training.

Training

If you are going to train a Gemini, you will have to catch him between appointments as he dashes off to chat with friends or dances around a tree.

The Gemini will enjoy an obedience class more than solitary training. He can handle distraction even if he is a distraction himself. He will love gossiping with the other pupils. His need to converse may cause problems, as you will have trouble getting his attention. Other trainers may resent you because he's such an amusing, witty guy that their dogs will be enthralled and break training. A Gemini is also a great mimic, and may be the main attraction with his charm.

Gemini is the sign of quick thinkers. They are eager to know too much too fast. They tend to skim through training, always ready to move on to a new command, and perhaps not learning thoroughly.

Your Gemini dog will be able to do more than one thing at a time. There may also be a tendency to drop what he is doing and move over to some other students to have a powwow.

23

He's versatile and adaptable and regimentation stifles him.

Gemini usually acts like he is always right, but he will change in his own fashion. He may try to bluff his way through some training exercises, and he is not famous for his patience.

Gemini will get your commands quickly the first time, but he probably won't pay attention to repeats. It may be hard to keep his attention if he is unwilling to persist with a drill.

Your Gemini will make you proud as he executes your first command with quick understanding. You will beam at him as the rest of the class flounders. Your pleasure may fade when the drill is repeated. He may just sit there and give you a "I already did that" look. Worse yet, he may leave your side to check out a bush. Well, at least he did it once.

Gemini eyes are always busy darting around looking for excitement. There is an air of electricity and nervous tension around him. He seems to be waiting to explode. He will have his nose in everything, including his neighbors' business. The Gemini is a public oriented pooch.

Public Relations

The Gemini will be popular. He's nosy, chatty, and a versatile friend to all. He'd love to be a mailman or a newspaper reporter. Spreading the news is his favorite pastime.

The Gemini will have quick mood changes, but he'll usually be sympathetic. His inconsistency is due to his nervous energy, and he just can't help speaking to everyone where ever he goes.

Gemini is a youthful sign. A Gemini dog needs to be sure he doesn't over-strain his nervous system, in spite of his youthful looks and actions. He'll need lots of sleep to restore energy, but his problem may be that he suffers from insomnia. It takes him a while before he can unwind into slumber.

Gemini needs fresh air and sunlight as well as rest. He is susceptible to illnesses of the nervous system and bronchial area. He may be accident prone due to his lively activity. Gemini may also be subject to infections of the paws. Check his feet after walking in the country.

If you try to keep him calm, remember that he is more likely to have a nervous breakdown from boredom than from over-activity.

As a parent, Gemini will be nosy about his pups' activities. A Gemini mom can be very involved in parenting and will encourage her pups to be as witty and lively as she is.

Gemini's emotions may be well hidden, and his intenseness may make him a little hard to get close to. You may have to spend some time calming him down first.

He doesn't need to be a one man or a one woman dog. He may be able to balance his loyalty between a couple or an entire family and have energy to burn. If you can keep up with him, you'll meet and talk with everyone in his world.

One single owner of a Gemini met all the people in her new apartment complex due to her socially accomplished dog. Being with a Gemini may be better than having your own social director.

Notes on Your Gemini Dog

The Puppy _____
_____
_____
_____
_____
_____
_____

Training _____
_____
_____
_____
_____
_____

Public Relations _____
_____
_____
_____
_____

Cancer

Cancer

June 22-July 22
Element—Water
Symbol—The Crab
Polarity—Yin, Feminine
Ruling Planet—Moon

The Puppy

If you picked a Cancer puppy, or she picked you, you were probably sold by her expressive eyes. They looked deep into your heart and stayed there.

Your Cancer pup has the strongest emotional needs of any Sun sign. She'll be very dependent on the reactions of her new family. She must be cuddled, adored, and approved of, as rejection will crush her delicate spirit.

She seems docile and quiet at first, but Cancer is a leadership sign—gentle leadership. She will have lovely manners, but she is not a follower.

Cancer will appear easy to manage and discipline as a pup, but you'll notice she usually gets her own way. She may become slightly spoiled if you are sensitive to her emotions. She becomes sad when ignored or spoken to harshly, so you may be inclined to pamper her a bit.

Having a Cancer companion has many benefits. She can be left by herself for hours if she's in the home that she loves. She won't chew up your clothing or nibble the furniture. Just be sure you let her know you appreciate her patience when you return.

Cancer's ruling planet is the Moon and your little water sign crab will change moods quickly. She may not be too easy to get along with even when at her sensitive, sympathetic best. She may be kind and a little home-maker, but then she will turn moody or snappy for no apparent reason, refusing to communicate.

Don't feel guilty. It's probably nothing that you have done. It may be the phase of the moon, or perhaps it has been raining. Your little crab may not be aware of what has caused her depression.

Cancer puppies love home and she won't be tempted to wander like Scorpio or Sagittarius. She's domestic and easily hurt. She is really timid and reticent at times, and staying home may be an excuse to hide many fears or phobias.

It is best to begin handling her fears while she is a puppy, or you may have an insecure dog on your hands. Love is the most important ingredient in her childhood. Love and sympathy are your calling cards to her heart.

She can dream up hurt or rejection all by herself, so begin work on her self-image early. She needs emotional support, so don't laugh at her fears or moods.

One Cancer pup was terrified of belts. If her owner took off a belt to hang it in the closet, the little Cancer was already under the bed, terror-stricken. The owner tried letting her sniff the belt, or leaving belts on the floor for her to investigate. Cancer refused to relinquish her fear. This smart owner finally accepted the fear and removed her belts in private. The fear could never be traced to an incident involving a belt, but perhaps as a tiny puppy this Cancer found the wrong end of one.

Cancers have fantastic memories, longer than most signs. Unusual behavior or phobias may be a result of an incident which occurred long before she was a part of your family.

Your little crab will be a great collector of memorabilia. This may include old bones and other chewables hidden under a bush or your couch.

One industrious Cancer had twelve tennis balls under a king-sized bed. Her owner wondered how she got twelve tennis balls when she didn't even play the game.

27

Cancer won't give up any treasured object. This is the puppy who will hang by her teeth, attached to a sock you'd like to get back.

Cancer puppies will retreat if hurt, and won't come around for days. They won't try to get even, but their self-imposed isolation in the dog house will make you feel like you are in the dog house yourself.

Cancer will be over-emotional at times and hypersensitive. Try to remember that if she doesn't get enough affection and approval as a pup, she may harden her heart in self-defense as an adult.

A Cancer never goes directly after what she wants. She'll probably prance around in all directions and then go for what she desires while you are not looking. Her changeable nature may keep you jumping, but don't despair. Cancer is easy to train if discipline is soft, the Moon is right, and it hasn't been raining. Good luck.

Training

Your Cancer has an incredible memory. She has been recording every event in her life since she was born. She is ready to learn even if she is a little confused or moody.

One thing in your favor is her desire to complete projects. More than any other sign, she likes to finish what is started. If you begin an exercise on Monday, don't start another until it is conquered and completed. This may mean a steady diet of one training command until the end of the week.

Cancer will need a calm working climate, but her excellent memory will never fail either of you. Her careful, calculated actions make her a reliable student.

Criticism must be handled carefully. She is sensitive to criticism and also very critical of herself. Let's hope you have worked on her self-image as a puppy.

You must keep a delicate balance in discipline. If you are too firm you can damage her sensitive nature. If treated harshly, your Cancer will pass on her treatment to others in the form of resentment. She may indulge in treeing the neighborhood cats or snarling at strangers. She needs lots of understanding or she may lose her compassionate gentleness and be bitter, brooding, and filled with self-pity.

In a training situation, a Cancer may tend to daydream occasionally or appear stubborn. Her good memory should improve her education as well as her concern for the opinion of friends and family. She doesn't like to let anyone down.

Never tease her. She won't show the hurt, but Cancers can become deeply depressed if ridiculed.

Your Cancer is like a personal mirror. She will reflect your emotions and may build a hard exterior if her public is not gentle.

Public Relations

The Cancer dog tends to be a worrier. She will worry by herself, and tend not to let others in on her problems. Like the symbol of her sign, the crab, she may appear to have a hard shell on the outside, but she is soft and inhibited on the inside.

Cancer tends to soak up the emotions of others, and tension in her home may cause ulcers or depression. She can get bluer than any other sign. Usually her depressions are self-induced and brought on by her own inner fears.

Cancer health problems usually involve the chest, kidneys, bladder, or skin. There may also be digestive problems due to emotional upsets. If worry makes her ill, love and cheerfulness make her well.

Foods that are rich in calcium are recommended. She also needs frequent exercise. She may have a tendency to retain fluids in later years and you may need to restrict salt in her diet.

Your crab will have a long memory for old toys. Don't throw out her first squeezy ball, even if it has lost its noise maker. She will also remember all names and faces and other parts of the anatomy. Once sniffed, information is recorded for life. She would be a good hotel manager, but, unfortunately, she will not be good in a crisis as stress gives her an upset stomach.

Cancer is a motherhood sign. As a parent Cancer will put family first. She won't like to see her puppies grow up and will try to keep her family together. She will be very protective of her young and may become fierce and aggressive if she feels her pups are in danger. Despite her protective confidence, if confronted herself, she will not fight to defend herself, only her pups. Her extreme involvement with her pups may make her touchy, so be gentle. This will be a very emotional time.

The inevitable departure of the pups may result in depression in a Cancer mom. This is a time for compassion. Respect her emotions and let sadness run its course.

If the breed permits, most Cancer dogs will love water. A refreshing swim may do wonders for the Cancer's nervous system.

Your Cancer companion may seem like a paradox. She swings between moods of kindness and protectiveness and then into bad tempered depression. She will often show you her hard exterior, but wish you would see the softness inside. She will be cautious and resourceful in one minute and then switch to self-pity and remorse.

Regardless of her moodiness, she loves the family. Her best side will always surface amid her loved ones.

She will cling to a personal relationship with you regardless of your manner or your Sun sign. After all, she chose you, didn't she?

The Puppy _____
_____
_____
_____
_____
_____

Training _____
_____
_____
_____
_____
_____

Public Relations _____
_____
_____
_____
_____
_____

Leo

Leo
The
Lion

Leo

July 23-August 22
Element — Fire
Symbol — The Lion
Polarity — Yang, Masculine
Ruling Planet — Sun

The Puppy

The first thing you will notice about Leo puppies is their dignity. Those with a lion sign have a regal bearing, and they will present themselves like young monarchs.

Depending on your own Sun sign, you may be very attracted to a royal litter. Their lofty antics make them a joy to any breeder, if not to their mother.

Once home, your reigning monarch will graciously accept attention and flattery from your family and friends. He will soon wrap all his subjects around his tiny paw.

He must have a kingdom somewhere, and if it is not at home, you will find him claiming dominion over the neighborhood pets. He needs to be a leader, or he will be hurt and sulk. He will tend to boss other pets in your home and may need to be restrained gently. Never reprimand him harshly in front of others. If crossed publicly he may roar like a lion or broodingly withdraw.

He will remain sunny, happy, and playful if he gets his own way. He will need to be trained to respect others as a puppy so that his fun-loving, playful nature does not become intolerant or dogmatic.

Leo pups are ambitious and enthusiastic, but not ruthless. Careful handling and guidance are necessary because a Leo pup may feel he is the only one of importance in a group. He really acts like he thinks he is splendid. He is, but he also has a tiny little doubt about it. Criticism can dampen his enthusiasm.

Leo has the power, will, and determination of Aries. The royal king is kind to his public, even if he appears a little pompous or snobbish.

A Leo puppy usually has two speeds: very fast, and slow. He may seem more restless and active than most. Then he will switch to a lazy Leo act and lie around sleeping. Leave him alone to recharge.

During his active periods he'll have great enthusiasm and high spirits. He will need his freedom. At these times he can bring sunshine and laughter into everyones' life. Leo, born to lead, loves parties and may form many neighborhood groups.

He may be intolerant or patronizing of other dogs and people at times, but he has warm-hearted charm. If he is approached as the neighborhood king, your chances for his friendship are good.

Even if your Leo seems to be a bit conceited at times, he is sensitive and easily hurt. He will never openly show that he has been offended. He will have a flair for the dramatic. You can tell by the lift of his nose and the gait of his walk when he leaves a humiliating situation that his pride has been damaged.

Leo is creative with a gift of showmanship. He will love being flattered and appreciated. With this attitude he will be fun to train. After all, how often do you get a chance to teach royalty?

Training

Before training your Leo you need to be aware of some of his own educational opinions. Leo has a long memory and often a closed mind. Once decisions are made he tends to stick with them. After all, a king is seldom wrong. Unlike Cancer, he will not waste his time or energy worrying about his ideas or performance.

Leo will be deeply involved in his education. He loves to work at his highest level. He will not be a quick thinker, but he arrives steadily at his goals. Leo will often believe he is more capable than other classmates. If he is enrolled in a formal obedience program, other students will need to acknowledge his superiority. Beware Scorpio and Aries.

Leo will need praise and applause. If ignored or disciplined harshly, he may seek the attention he needs by indulging in poor behavior or forcing issues.

One Leo, when frustrated by his owner's lack of approval and attention in class, mistook his owner's leg for a fire hydrant. Results were disastrous.

31

The lion does have a sense of the dramatic, and he loves to be the center of attention. He will do things in a big way. Leo will be a bit extravagant, but he will work hard.

The lion loves to organize people and pets and he may try to take over a training class. Most professional trainers are aware of Leo's needs. Smart teachers will appeal to his pride and love of flattery. Leo may love to show off, but he will do so with dignity. He is not maliciously aggressive, he just loves to lead the parade. If he has had proper upbringing as a pup he will soon see he needs to allow others to have a turn.

Your lion will suffer if his training is dull or boring. He needs to express his natural enthusiasm and exuberance.

Leo may at times be a little lazy about training and try to charm his way out of discipline or routine. Appeal to his vanity and love of superiority. Gentle, continuous discipline with lots of love is best.

He will learn fast if he wants to, and be generous with his knowledge. Leos are noted for being generous. A Leo will share almost anything with his classmates. One generous lion was willing to share his leash, collar and charm as he pranced around a cute little Capricorn. He was regally offended when her owner was not overjoyed. Some people don't know when they have been honored.

Whatever the outcome, Leo's charm and generosity will be a plus in the public relations department.

Leos have good recuperative powers and their physical strength is usually good. Leos rule the heart. Some dogs with the lion sign may develop heart problems or high blood pressure with age. Due to their enthusiasm, they often forget that bodies get tired. When Leo finally takes a rest, he needs it.

Leo is the father sign as Cancer is the mother sign. Leo will be very proud of his puppies and be an enthusiastic parent. Female Leos tend to be overly domineering mothers and a little bossy.

Leo loves to conquer. Male Leos have been known to hunt the opposite sex with great vigor. Leo's sparkling eyes may also notice the opposite sex much sooner than other signs. The teen-aged Romeo of the neighborhood is probably a Leo.

Leo loves important duties. Getting the morning paper will give him a sense of authority, especially if he is well-appreciated. The routine guarding of the back porch may be boring and very unrewarding for a Leo.

Most of all, your Leo needs to look up to and respect his family. If he respects you, you will have a loyal, affectionate, expressive companion for as long as he lives. He will be a willing slave, especially if his work is interesting.

Try to remember that behind his roar, Leo is pretending to be brave, but is a tiny bit afraid he isn't. Your love and approval will keep his precious dignity intact.

It can be fun living with a furry king.

Public Relations

You must have noticed Leo's pleased look as strangers stop to admire him. He loves attention and will hold court at every opportunity. He will have an air of dignity even if he is covered with mud or stuck in a trash can. Although his regal ways make him popular and sought after, his pride can be a handicap. He may react violently if scolded or humiliated in front of his public. Best to lead him quietly aside and speak firmly into his ear.

Although most Leos seem to be cheerful extroverts, if not a little pushy, there is a second variety that appears withdrawn, quiet, and almost timid. The second type of Leo is usually the result of too strict discipline and lack of approval. If his spirit has been dampened, an unhappy adult Leo is usually the result. Unfortunately, it will be Leo himself who will decide how much discipline is too much and when he hasn't received enough praise. He can be his own worst enemy.

The Puppy _____
_____
_____
_____
_____
_____
_____

Training _____
_____
_____
_____
_____
_____
_____

Public Relations _____
_____
_____
_____
_____
_____

Virgo

Virgo

August 24-September 23
Element — Earth
Symbol — The Virgin
Polarity — Yin, Feminine
Ruling Planet — Mercury

The Puppy

Did you pick out the puppy with the slightly worried look? Perhaps you were attracted to her neat appearance. She was clean as a whistle and sat modestly as you discussed her price. On the way home she was quiet and seemed preoccupied with some inner problem.

As a puppy she will be alert and quick, yet more peaceful than most signs. She is meticulous to a fault, and very fussy about her food. Even as a hungry pup, a Virgo will slide her little nose through her dinner and push all unacceptable food into one neat pile. She will daintily select her favorite tidbits.

Virgo will prefer the same dish, in the exact spot where she wants it. This may involve pushing her dish around chairs to her own place on the floor.

Virgo will be fussy about her bedding too. A Virgo puppy can spend an hour arranging her rug or pillow just so. She won't sleep until it is perfect.

You might begin to wonder if you are in for a hard time, but she won't be moody or aggressive about her desires. She will very correctly go about adjusting her world to order. She is neat, tidy, and organized in the little details that concern her. She probably won't expect you to change, she'll just reorder after you have left her on her own.

Virgo will be quiet and subdued in crowds or large parties, but more open and friendly in the family.

She will mind readily and may have a tendency to imitate other dogs if there are any in her home.

As a puppy, Virgo will require very little discipline. She only needs to be gently corrected, and if you are stern or angry she may worry herself into illness. She is a serious little virgin with a dependable, friendly disposition.

She will need to be shown her error only once when she has made a puppy blunder. She will quickly overcome her mistake as she aims to please. Training too early may make her nervous and worried. Virgo will not question your authority like Scorpio, so let her enjoy her puppyhood.

Your little Virgo will need a lot of affection, but she may not show her need. She is not dependent like Pisces, but under that stolid little nature, she'd love to be hugged.

In addition to being a little fuss-budget and finicky about her appearance, your Virgo will love routine and detail. She will easily adjust to your work and family schedule. She will love regular meal times, although she may pick at the food. She will need a daily walk schedule. Virgo will be an easy puppy to house-break if you are gentle and she doesn't worry herself into an upset.

The little virgin is a constant doer. Her need to be busy, busy, busy, may be a little comical. If she's not arranging her water dish or fixing her bed, she will be arranging a soft place in your garden or cleaning her paws. She loves detail work.

Although she may appear to be preoccupied by a serious problem, she is not day dreaming like a Libra. She is sorting, or nit-picking some detail in her surroundings.

Virgo is really a little love. Don't forget to interrupt her detailed concerns and pick her up for a cuddle or a short talk. She will love you for it and feel more secure as you start her education.

Training

In training, Virgo will be alert and willing. She needs routine. She has an inquiring mind and won't always accept your discipline, but if your training commands seem reasonable she will be happy to please.

If you enroll Virgo in a professional training class, she won't be the leader. She likes to stay in the background. She will provide stability and a sense of class to her colleagues, but she needs the security of a supporting role. If your little Virgo does become the class president, check her moon sign. There probably is an Aries or a Leo in there some place.

Virgo may have some possibilities as a show dog. She will stay immaculately groomed and compliant in position. Still, large crowds intimidate her, so check her other signs and breeding first.

Virgo has high intelligence and a love of good workmanship.

Once she begins her training, she may be such a perfectionist that she becomes too high-strung to perform. She is overly critical. Again, lots of love and encouragement will help, as well as a look at her other signs.

She will tend to be overwhelmed by complicated instructions, so give commands one-at-a-time. Don't let her know when the training finals occur because she would worry needlessly. She knows her stuff, but is insecure, and wants to be perfect.

Virgos have a great deal of nervous energy. Keep moving so she doesn't have time to worry. If she is enrolled in a training class, keep her occupied during breaks.

She may appear rather standoffish to the other students. This is in your favor. Her naturally prudish nature will keep her from being distracted by a socially minded Leo. Her reservation can be charming as she obeys your commands with precision. She will need lots of encouragement to perform well. She has a basic sense of inferiority that only your approval can adjust.

Because she is a creature of habit and loves schedules, the more often you include her education in your daily routine, the quicker she will respond. Her confidence will improve as well.

Virgo may be just the companion you need to keep you on time. At precisely 5:02 she will arrive with brush in mouth to remind you that it is grooming time. She will love to be brushed, and will let you know if you miss any spots.

Virgo's main goal will be service, and she is a hard worker. If she is a bit picky, just smile and relax as she licks her paws again and adjusts her collar.

After she has researched the class, and analyzed your commands, she will be ready to perform for you and her public.

Public Relations

Your Virgo will try to please if she knows what is expected. Although her privacy is an important part of her life, she likes to be included in your day. If her routine is upset, she will worry.

The Virgo pet may have problems with digestion, especially if she is concerned. Her fussy eating habits will not allow her to gain weight in later years.

She may be prone to dandruff or skin eruptions from time to time. She is the champion of the nervous itch. She loves to be cleaned and bathed, but watch your shampoos for irritants. She has delicate skin.

Tension affects her health in the form of ulcers or hypochondria. Her own concern over little things may cause health problems. One Virgo pooch, when encountering live-in guests—fleas—became so involved in the habit and detail of search and seizure in her fur, that even after she was dipped and certified flealess, she continued to hunt and peck her sensitive skin. Her face had that worried, preoccupied look so well known to the Virgo.

Virgo will be a realistic, mature dog. She is very practical and a bit of a loner at times. Close emotional relationships with you or your family may be difficult at times because she finds it hard to express her love.

Virgo will be a somewhat difficult parent because of her desire for neatness and propriety, unless she is lucky enough to give birth to a litter of little Virgos. She may be over-critical or a little distant.

Virgos are almost snobs at times, and this should be kept in mind for breeding. The Virgo—especially the female—needs time to approve of her mate. A sudden venture may lead to absolute rejection on her part.

Although your Virgo may seem a little vain at times, she is dependable and sincere. Fastidious in her grooming, and detailed in her behavior, she makes a good supportive companion. If your home needs organization and a sympathetic ear, she's your dog.

The Puppy

_____
_____
_____
_____
_____

Training

_____
_____
_____
_____
_____

Public Relations

_____
_____
_____
_____

Libra

Libra

September 24-October 23
Element — Air
Symbol — The Scales
Polarity — Yang, Masculine
Ruling Planet — Venus

The Puppy

If you were chosen by the Libra puppy, you are in for a gentle upbringing. If you acquired your puppy at a kennel and met all his siblings, you may have noticed that the entire group was well-mannered. A proud mother watched over a group of model puppies with a twinkle in her eye.

Maybe she knows something you don't.

When you brought your model puppy home you may have noticed that loud or sudden noises seemed to startle him. The Libra pooch lives in a world of delicate equilibrium. He may appear to be high strung, and strange noises upset him.

He loves harmony in all aspects of life, and especially sound. It is not surprising that any Libra dog enjoys soft, calming music. He prefers classical, and perhaps a few oldies, but no hard rock or jazz. After an exhausting day you could enjoy this with him. Music is a must if you are going to leave pooch alone inside for a while. Be sure you are certain of the channel selection. He is a born aristocrat.

The Libra needs a lot of peace, quiet, and rest, especially as a puppy. If you are a multi-dog family, or there are other creatures living in the house, be sure he has his own space and, again, the music, softly.

He may appear a little lazy, but your Libra pup will play energetically for hours, and then collapse into a serene little ball. He isn't erratic; he is just balancing.

He is gathering his energy for the next busy spurt of prancing puppyhood.

One Libra pup, after a busy weekend of camping, boating, and nights filled with howling coyotes, returned home to sleep for two days. He wouldn't wake up to eat. After recharging his batteries, he was up and at it again.

The Libra puppy can literally charm the socks off anyone. He can wiggle anything he wants out of you with his lovely manners and gentle, winning ways. He is also very polite.

Libra is such a charmer, and so well behaved, that you might be tempted to spoil him. Don't pamper your puppy or he may have problems with discipline in his training sessions.

Your puppy will be gentle and affectionate with children, especially if he has time to rest between play periods. Put him down in his own private sleeping spot when the children nap. The children might like soft music too.

Libra hates violence in any form, so speak gently to the pup and no harsh scolding.

You may have to watch the Libra puppy's diet because he has a delicate balance system. His digestive tract may react poorly to emotional upsets or eating in a hurry. He hates to do anything in a hurry, as you will soon find out.

Libra is really a careful little fellow, and depending on his breed, he may be actually timid. His love of harmony requires him to be gentle with himself and others.

He can't cope with dirt, or unpleasant surroundings, so be sure his private living-area is immaculate and he will help to keep it clean. His love of elegance and refinement is evident even as a puppy in his choice of music, grooming, and comfort.

Your little Libra will be neat and clean and on the whole, a real joy. He is a well-behaved friend if you understand his need for moderation in all things. You may even find yourself being more relaxed as you respect his ways.

So, on to the training of the gentle gentleman.

Training

Training must begin with just you and your Libra. He doesn't want the cheering crowds which an Aries adores, and he also has a problem making up his mind. Did you think he was slow or stubborn as a pup? Not at all. He is indecisive, easily distracted, and terribly afraid of making a mistake. With this in mind, begin your training when he is well-rested. Find a quiet place with no loud or sudden noises. There should be no motorcycles or traffic of any kind. If another dog or person approaches your secluded training area, be prepared for

39

him to completely lose his concentration. He is easily distracted by an audience.

This all may sound very difficult, but he does aim to please. If you can keep his attention in a gentle, loving way, he will quickly learn all the basic commands. Don't expect him to perform for your friends, as he may be too busy charming them to hear your instructions.

His problem of indecision can be easily controlled by using simple, gentle commands. Give each command in a calm voice. Do not repeat any command; he has heard you. He is not being stubborn. Libra is making the decision to follow the command and to do it right. He hates mistakes, and in the long run, this makes him an excellent student. For instance, he will not be sloppy on his turns when heeling.

Please don't take personally his slowness to respond to you. He is not challenging your authority like Scorpio. He is weighing a delicate equilibrium within himself. After some practice, the lag-time between your command and his response will shorten. He will be more confident of himself and your directions. You may be also.

If he does not respond immediately, don't repeat your instructions. He doesn't function well when he feels pressured. He may not be able to concentrate if he is rushed. Libra will become confused if two commands are given together. Let him complete one first before giving another.

It will be very confusing for a Libra if two people are training him at once. He may become stubborn, refuse to move, or be hyperactive. He is easily influenced.

Libra may take so long to decide what to do that you may think he doesn't know the response, but his slowness may be a blessing. You will have time to catch him before he makes a mistake.

One lovable Libra was trained separately every day for weeks and responded beautifully in uncomplicated conditions. However, upon joining a training class, he threw schooling to the wind. He became so busy with the other dogs—charming his way into hearts, and taking telephone numbers—that he completely forgot his owner. He didn't hear a single command. He was quite dismayed when his owner removed him from the training field, but returned quickly to perfect obedience in the absence of his classmates.

Your Libra will usually try to keep himself under control, and he is learning to cope with his indecision and social problems. He may appear to be procrastinating, but be fair. He will be sensitive to the give and take of the training relationship.

Well, you have a friendly companion, and, with patience and understanding, he will be able to handle distraction and crowds. This will be a plus in the public relations department since your elegant and flirtatious Libra may attract all kinds of attention from his public.

Public Relations

Your reluctant diplomat may seem a little confusing. He loves people, but he doesn't like crowds. Crowds are just too much for his sensitive balance to contend with for long. He may sit by your side with a glazed look in his eyes or run from person to person, wagging himself into a frenzy. He loves attention, but only in small doses.

He does make a great host for your home. As a puppy he will be extremely affectionate and enthusiastic about your friends. As he matures, he will remain lovable but may be more reserved as he grows into his refined nature.

By the way, he is a born strategist, and once he decides what he wants, he will usually get it.

Some Libras may be inclined to overeat. You will have to be his balancing element in that area. His kidneys are his delicate area. Be sure he always has plenty of cool water in his clean, decorated dish. Peppermint leaves—if he'll eat a few—are good for indigestion and purifying the breath.

If your Libra gets ill, he will require lots of rest. Don't be surprised by his ability to sleep for marathon lengths of time. He will need his naps all his life as this period of inner harmony allows him to adjust his Libra scales.

Libras try to stay neat and clean, but this will depend on the breed. It is hard to be neat when nature is causing you to shed all over your quarters or when you need to be clipped.

Libras love water, especially if they have been bred for water sports or hunting. If a Libra is lucky enough to be a water dog, he will race you to the pond and, when in it, he will stay afloat for hours.

Libras usually are very graceful even if they have big, shaggy bodies. Watching a Libra run can be poetry in motion.

He has a sweet disposition with an air of purity and innocence about him. When people first meet him, they feel he is safe and not a nipper or a scrapper.

The most amazing quality of a Libra is his ability to absorb your temperament. If you are nervous or upset, he will pick up on it. If you are happy he will wiggle from tail to nose.

Your Venus-ruled Libra has a great love of elegance and refinement. If female, she will be very classy, sophisticated, and also a little flirtatious. Be prepared to fight off the neighborhood males, for she is impressionable and easily taken advantage of.

Any Libra dog should be a good companion because Libra is the sign of partnerships. The Libra hates confrontations and upsets, and may try to be all things to all people to keep the peace.

His compassionate heart will make him a sensitive companion. Just be sure he gets lots of rest if you are on an emotional roller coaster ride. He will need time to balance the both of you.

The Puppy _____

Training _____

Public Relations _____

Scorpio

Scorpio

October 24-November 22
Element — Water
Symbol — The Scorpion or The Eagle
Polarity — Yin, Feminine
Ruling Planets—Pluto/Mars

The Puppy

"Oh, my," your friends said with a giggle, "A Scorpio puppy."

You probably hadn't given Sun signs too much thought. You were too busy admiring her sturdy, little body and her serious, intent gaze. That is what sold you on your pet, and it is all a part of the fabulous Scorpio kit.

The entire litter will be husky and strong for their breed. There will be no runt with Scorpio pups.

That powerful little body and piercing, intelligent gaze have another partner—willfulness. Your little scorpion has the will and sense of purpose of a gladiator. Intensity is her name and game. She has powerful feelings and will live life to the fullest, every glorious, romping minute.

Your best bet is to keep her busy. She will need to release her high-powered emotional energy. With proper guidance, perhaps, she will not release it in destructive ways, such as tearing up your slippers.

She is aggressive, and loves robust sports played either with you, other dogs, children, or your lawn furniture and favorite plants.

You will need to approach her with firm kindness. Don't wait for six or nine months for training. Discipline must start the day you meet your Scorpio pooch. This does not mean formal training or tricks. That will come later. From day one, you must begin to let your puppy know two facts: she is the puppy, and you are the master. She will question this repeatedly. She will respect you and learn from you if she knows you are strong. This means matching her will. Good luck!

She will need to learn to respect your authority at an early age or any training later is impossible. All this may sound rather threatening, but she is worth it. When she matures she will be very loyal, intelligent, and courageous, and a great family protector. Your little Scorpio is a lady who does not know compromise. She needs to try to be boss, and her defiant gaze when scolded may send you running for your rolled up newspaper, or two aspirins. Don't give in. Be firm with your rules. Make sure your rules are appropriate to her age and that she understands what is required. Continue to be firm with your little dictator. Perseverance is the word, but don't be harsh or cruel. In spite of her need for constant discipline, she needs love too.

Avoid being nervous or lenient in discipline. If she gets away with jumping up on the couch once, she will be harder to convince the second time. She will be looking for your weak spot. Don't let her passionate nature catch you off guard. She needs to know you will not weaken, yet she will test you again and again. Your best bet is to be confident that you are fair and then stick to your guns. This may be your best chance to practice your assertiveness training.

Be sure you are loving with your discipline, or she may become fearful. There is a delicate balance to her willpower. She may be inclined to have extreme highs and lows of emotional energy, and excessive discipline may frighten her.

Scorpio will have a cute little habit of hiding her toys, or even your socks or other private clothing. She cherishes her own secrets. This really isn't too much to tolerate. She needs a few hiding places and also her own private place to sleep. Hopefully she will hide her bones in the yard and not in your laundry basket, but she must have her privacy.

Speaking of privacy, woe to any other animal that chews her bones. She is very possessive. If there are other animals in the home, it may be wise to warn them or be sure each has its own area and dish.

Scorpio is possessive of her things, and you may be one of them. It is easier to tolerate her jealous nature if you remember that her possessive manner can be channeled into excellent guard dog material. On the other hand, her stubborn streaks need a little work.

The scorpion is a born dictator. It may not seem fair that she has her secrets but you can't: anything you appear to be hiding will appeal to her. Paper bags, closets, waste baskets, garbage cans, cabinets, hold intrigue and tantalize the Scorpio. For her own safety, inspect any area she could possibly get into, and remove poisons or valuables. Her inclination to "poke around" is in contrast to her own need for secrecy and mystery.

By now you will have learned that she has an intense temperament, but she can learn to control herself if you are strong. If you have been persistent and convinced her that you are the authority, she will be ready for obedience training.

I'll bet you thought the time would never come.

Training

You have been in training for her training for months. A professional training class will probably be best. If you have done your home work with love and dedication, the worst is over.

Scorpio has a brilliant mind and lots of personality and courage. She will be a hard worker and can handle long training periods.

Scorpio also needs to feel important. All that power, when properly channeled, gives her great endurance.

Her education needs to be exciting and varied. She hates dullness. An hour of commands of "Sit," "Stay," or "Down," may bore her to distraction and restlessness, leading to trouble. Unlike Capricorn, Scorpio is quick to adapt to new commands and can easily change goals.

Scorpio can be tops in her class, but remember to keep her physically active every day. She needs to work off all her energy to keep her curiosity from getting her into trouble. If she has had a lazy day, her detective nature may drive her to see how much excitement she can cause in training class, or she may just have to investigate that bush which is on the opposite side of the field.

A Scorpio of a small breed may appear calm, but there is a tremendous amount of emotional energy boiling on the inside. If she is kept inside most of the time, this energy may surface in shoe-chewing, magazine-ripping or waste basket searches. If she is from a larger breed—a herder or a hunter—she will need even more opportunities for physical exercise.

Scorpio will be a determined student. Be sure you give her lots of approval when she performs. Like the Aries, she seems not to need your praise, but she secretly thrives on it. If she meets with constant disapproval or failure, she may become depressed.

A Scorpio will guess your feelings—just like a Pisces—but she will be more direct in letting you know she knows. Keep the faith. You have a winner with powerful, animal magnetism.

Public Relations

Your Scorpio dog hates secrets. You cannot sneak in with a doggie bag, planned for your own breakfast. She wants her goodies now. She loves rich food and may over-indulge. Her suspicious nature may cause her to investigate her dish like a royal food taster, but she will love table scraps and fattening delicacies. Scorpio will be blunt and direct in her behavior, but at least you will know where you stand.

Scorpio can stand great pain. Be sure to check her for ticks and paw splinters often, for she may not let you know when she hurts. Grin-and-bear-it may be a detrimental attitude for her.

The scorpion may weaken with any excess or overwork, but she quickly recuperates. Rest and love are her best healers. She may have sensitive skin and require careful brushing and bathing.

Her weak areas could be urinary problems, or disorders involving the reproductive organs. This will depend on her breed and specific heredity.

Scorpio will be extremely loyal to your family but she can be a little hard on strangers. She can get quite nasty to people or pets she doesn't consider part of her home. Scorpio will make a great guard dog, and her loyalty and courage will always protect you. Since she is loyal to you, she will expect you to be loyal to her. She will not approve of your petting and cuddling other dogs in her presence. If you stop to pet a neighborhood dog, you will be sniffed thoroughly when you return home. Dog hair on your slacks is considered to be a breach of loyalty.

Your own emotional climate will affect Scorpio. Arguments or outbursts in the home will upset her, and she may need to go off to her private corner. Scorpio is the Psychologist of the Dog World. She will analyze your moods.

Your Scorpio may be a bit of a flirt. If you have a male Scorpio, be prepared for a few paternity suits, or at least a few fights. The opposite sex intrigues the scorpion. Remember what was said about curiosity? It may have killed the cat, but not your Scorpio. Her passionate nature and tendency to over-indulge usually affects her sexual affairs. She has a strong sex drive, and is attractive to other Sun signs. She appears exciting, dynamic, and mysterious to the pooch next door.

Scorpios often have large litters, and may have some problems with delivery. As a parent, a Scorpio will be strict, but willing to enjoy her pups' zest for life.

Scorpio dogs have a tendency to create, and then destroy their creation. A good example of this was a Dalmation who enjoyed digging huge holes in the yard. When he completed hole number one, it was usually filled by dirt flying from holes two and three. This trait can have its advantages.

Your Scorpio will be a challenge and a definite presence in your home. Although a blunt nuisance, or an occasionally over-energetic governess, when she is curled at your feet she is the ideal friend and protector. Can you ask for more?

Notes on Your Scorpio Dog

The Puppy

_____
_____
_____
_____
_____
_____

Training

_____
_____
_____
_____
_____
_____

Public Relations

_____
_____
_____
_____
_____

Saggitarius

Sagittarius

November 23-December 21
Element — Fire
Symbol — The Archer/half-man, half-horse
Polarity — Yang, Masculine
Ruling Planet — Jupiter

The Puppy

A litter of Sagittarius puppies will act like a group of tiny archers, all shooting in different directions.

Your Sagittarius puppy will miss his litter-mates when he arrives at your home. He, more than other signs, needs his friends. He'll be very open and playful, but don't leave him alone for long. His need for companionship may turn him into an early barker when left alone. Other undesirable habits like chewing everything that doesn't move, or whining, may occur. He may also take to pouting or sulking.

Your archer will love to sleep on your clothing. He will need to feel he is near you. Leave an old t-shirt where he sleeps, and you will find him curled up on top of it in the morning. Be wise and pick his security blanket early from your old clothing, or he may choose your best silk shirt. He will need his security blanket long after he is grown, as the Sagittarius has a tendency to remain the playful pup.

The fire sign dog needs lots of acknowledgement too, or he will droop and mope. Make a little fuss over him when you get home and applaud his puppy tricks.

Your Sagittarius will be a very curious little archer, and he will need to investigate his world, especially strange noises. He will love to go through the grocery bag with you and sniff each item. One happy Sagittarius has been known to empty entire cabinets and check out each item. Unfortunately, he hasn't been trained to put the contents back yet!

Sagittarius is very quick, and he will soon learn to identify all the sounds he has heard. If you rattle your house keys even slightly, his keen hearing will send him flying to the door to see where you are going.

The archer needs his freedom. He is an extrovert and very blunt about his independence. He loves adventure, and change is his middle name. He'll be rather wild as a pup, and good at games and rough-housing. He's boisterous, capricious, and may lack self-discipline.

Sagittarius loves a cause. He must have something of his own. As he matures, he may not need his security blanket, but he will require his own dish or spot in the family room. He may be very territorial, and if male, this will include stalking around his grounds daily. Heaven help any pooch who hikes on a bush in his yard. He is usually jovial and open-minded, but after all, it is his private area.

On the other hand, he may confuse what is his and what is yours. He may want to share your favorite chair or pillow.

One Sagittarius owner found she was missing some of her more personal clothing. Strange how her nylons seemed to turn up in the dog house.

Sagittarius may lead a carefree youth, filled with excitement and restlessness. He is unconventional. The archer will start several projects at once before he finishes anything. He will run from chewing his bone to chasing the cat, and then back to an unfinished evacuation under the garage. If you want to observe this trait, try throwing him two balls at once. He will probably not bring back either one.

Sagittarius always loves to develop his intellect, although it may not appear so. Beware. He will put all his investigations together later for further use.

The archer is claustrophobic and dislikes being enclosed in small places. Chains, leashes, and collars will not be to his liking. Break him in to a collar slowly, a few hours a day at first. Leashes will be easier to accept. He will know he is going somewhere new and interesting when he is on the other end of that restrictive leash. He will be happier if he is allowed to roam free in the yard rather than on a leash line. Just be sure you have a high fence or he will be on his way, with his head in the clouds.

47

You have already realized that your Sagittarius has a strong will, but he is intelligent, quick on his feet, and loves adventure. He is eager to put all his knowledge to work, so on with the training.

Training

Sagittarius will enjoy training because he has a bright mind and is naturally curious. He will be restless and you may have to work at getting his attention. He is very fond of other animals, so training needs to begin at home before going to a formal class.

Do not be too severe with him when he is a pup. He may be a little careless in his responses, but too much demand for precision or detail will dampen his incentive. He may question your authority—like Scorpio—but he will give in graciously if he is convinced you are logical. If your commands are fair, he will respect them and he can be depended upon to perform.

Sagittarius hates deception, so no tricks please. You can outsmart him, but he is so sincere and frank himself he won't understand why you hid his dish as a joke.

In an obedience class he will be a dapper sportsman. His problem is he doesn't like to concentrate on any one skill for too long. You may have to take him aside and change from heeling, off, leash, to sit, stays while the rest of the class goes on heeling. If he is bored, he will be very tactless about it and may harass the other owners or just go to sleep in the middle of training. He loves the excitement of change and will be cheerful and optimistic when you vary the routine.

Unlike Virgo, his lack of attention to detail may cause the Sagittarius to take some time before he polishes up his act. He will be in a hurry to get on to the next command. Once trained, he will be capable of a great deal of discipline. Advanced commands will be a challenge to him.

Sagittarius has a need for physical and mental exercise, so train him often. He's versatile, and will love advanced training classes because they will give him a chance to show off his talents and keep him around other animals. He is a social fellow and enjoys the attention of an audience.

Public Relations

A Sagittarius will always show you his feelings. He is extremely honest—blunt in his way. The Sagittarius dog tends to go to extremes or exaggerate. If you accidentally step on his tail he may go into a prolonged fit of yelping and dramatics. He may forget what happened before he is quiet.

He'll be rather sensitive at times. If he chooses to make a big fuss over your Aunt Emma—who only sees him once a year—don't feel put down. His enthusiasm tends to go to extremes, and he may momentarily forget the hand that feeds him. He will be generous with his love, and he will always try to cheer you up if you are blue.

His great love of people and their pets encourages his natural roaming instincts. He will be loyal to you, but he also needs to see what is down the street. Depending on his breed, you may have trouble keeping him home. Unlike Capricorn, whose home is his castle, your Sagittarius' heart will be at home, but his furry body may be elsewhere. Always be sure he has a collar on with your name and telephone number on the tag. His need to roam is built into his independent streak. If he is often alone, he may be tempted to wander more: plenty of family attention may curb this.

Sagittarius loves people, and he is blindly optimistic that they will return his affection. He can get into a temper if he is pushed around or rejected by people who abuse his friendship. He may be extremely crushed if someone finally slaps his friendly, wiggling body after repeatedly trying to discourage his advances.

Your Sagittarius will yelp in exaggerated anger when the mailman swings his bag at him. He will not realize that the poor man is dog-shy from bouts with a quarreling Capricorn. The man was not convinced by your Sagittarius' informal, honest approach.

The Sagittarius will usually have good health. Depending on his breed and heredity, he may be sensitive in the hips or legs. He may also be slightly accident-prone due to his impulsive moves and his love of outdoor and indoor sports.

He recuperates quickly, but seldom rests when he is ill. You may have to confine him if he is seriously ill, but be sure to keep in mind his need for companionship. He won't want to be isolated. Bring his little bed into the main part of the living area where he can watch you as he mends.

Sagittarius may overeat. He will have a tendency to go to extremes with food. If he is house-bound, do not give him too much food, as he may eat to compensate for his lack of freedom. He will not need routine in his feeding or exercise schedule as long as each is frequent, exciting, and new. Sagittarius may also love vegetables more than other signs do. Give him small amounts and watch his reactions.

As a parent, Sagittarius will have fun with the litter. He will romp and play like a pup and be outrageously enthusiastic about the whole experience.

Your Sagittarius is a big-hearted clown. He will be blindly devoted to you in his own manner. He may roam, but you are his lord and master. His direct manner will assure you that he is your archer forever.

48

Notes on Your Sagitarrius Dog

The Puppy _____
_____
_____
_____
_____
_____

Training _____
_____
_____
_____
_____
_____

Public Relations _____
_____
_____
_____
_____
_____

Capricorn

Capricorn

December 22-January 20
Element — Earth
Symbol — The Goat
Polarity — Yin, Feminine
Ruling Planet — Saturn

The Puppy

The Capricorn puppy was born mature. Whether she weighs two pounds or twenty, is shaggy or smooth, she will have the look of a little lady.

She is deliberate and certain of her every move and manner. With her stable, determined temperament, she will not exhibit the wiggling and bouncing behavior of some of the other Zodiac sign puppies. Some days—when she catches your eye with a patient stare—you may feel like you are the child.

She won't be fussy or hard to control when she is a puppy. She will bide her time and eventually get her own way in most puppy endeavors. Perseverance—in a quiet way—is the little goat's game.

Capricorn pups may fall into two varieties:

The Mountain Goat type will be climbing to greener pastures with an eye on the social set. Her reliable, careful, and persevering ways keep her steps always upward.

The Domestic Goat type will be ambitious too, but competition may be just too much of a drain. She will gravitate to a safe level in her world and will remain unruffled. Perhaps she will be a little rigid in her outlook, and at times be a bit of a "wet blanket." She is a rock of endurance and self control.

Your little goat loves routine. She is happiest and most secure when her activities are routine. She loves to be fed at the same time every day and in her same puppy dish. She likes her walk at the same time each evening. A break in her routine may cause her to be moody and stubborn. She likes you to follow a consistent schedule as well.

She can be shy and sweet, but she is wise beyond her years. She knows the hand that feeds her well.

Capricorn will be very polite and can be easily handled. You may discover that, after a fashion, she will end up with her own way. When she has chosen her spot to sleep, be prepared to rearrange your furniture to suit her.

She has infinite patience. Capricorn is seldom impulsive and never in a hurry, unless it suits her purpose. Don't let her slow deliberation fool you. She still likes to be in charge.

She is tenacious. You may also discover that she is jealous. She can show her jealousy in a variety of ways. Tempers may flare if the cat sniffs her dish or if you are on the phone so long she misses her routine puppy walk. Don't come home with dog hairs all over your sweater from some friend's pooch. She may sniff and snarl. And also you may notice jealousy rear its little green head on the training field. She'll need lots of security to overcome her possessive nature and retain her ambitious attitude.

With luck she will keep her sweet nature, unless she is pushed too far or trained too early.

Training

You may have noticed that your little Capricorn is very responsive to your demands. Her training will be easy, if you remember her love of routine and work with her stubbornness that surfaces occasionally.

51

Since she loves schedules, try to keep the training at the same time and in the same area. She will quickly add this new event to her well-planned routine and be very cooperative.

She can be entered in a professional training class. The other dogs and trainers won't interfere with her complete concentration and deliberation. She is not flighty.

Be sure that you give her one hundred percent of your attention in class. Remember her jealous streak? Don't ooh and ahh too loudly about the adorable antics of that cute little Libra. Your Capricorn needs the security of knowing she is in your spotlight.

Capricorn also likes the fame of the public eye, and her cool, calculating mind may eventually make her the center of attention. The goat appears to learn slowly, and may plod along, but what she learns she will never forget. Patience is the key to her training and it will pay off in the end. She will be obedient and reliable in the toughest situations. She will not disappoint you in front of friends, or during panic situations with other dogs. Capricorn will be dependable while other quicker dogs are running off after cats and cars.

During group training sessions, the more domestic Capricorn may seem quiet and timid. She may lack confidence and not mix with other dogs or owners. Her apparently slow, deliberate manner may seem to be a drawback, but in the long run she may be the valedictorian of her class because of her persistence.

One Capricorn student was left in a training class on a sit-stay command when her owner went to her car. Her owner met a friend and stopped to talk. As the class concluded and pooches and people filed out, the Capricorn sat resolutely still. That's perseverance.

Your little goat may have rare stubborn spells, especially if her routine is broken or she feels pushed. Her steadfast approach is not glamorous, but she often wins the race in her calm way. She will respect your authority. Her slowness to respond is deliberation, not the indecision of Libra.

She needs plenty of exercise, and may need to be encouraged to spend time in play outdoors. The best way to approach this is to consult her date book and work exercise into her schedule.

The mountain goat variety of Capricorns usually appear confident to others, although they may not be as totally in charge as they look. This Capricorn will be the dog in the class that knows where the fire plug is, and starts out with such a determined gait that the rest of the class follows.

Whether a mountain or domestic type, most Capricorns have the same style in public relations. Your goat will wait out all resistance to her plans. She may even out-wait you.

Public Relations

Your Capricorn pooch loves her home; it is her castle. She won't ever run off, and can be trusted to stay in her yard once she knows its boundaries. Unless her breed has a running or herding instinct, she will be happy to sit in her yard and observe.

Her attachment to her home may keep her indoors more often than not, and she may need to be encouraged to get fresh air.

She will be an excellent guard dog because of her love of home and family. She won't be distracted by a stray cat or a good looking Dachshund. She will be serious about her job and very complete. Her idea of family— her main delight —may extend beyond your immediate kin to close friends and the paper boy.

Capricorn's health will seem to improve with age. In her way she is an old puppy who will grow younger as she matures. She may be susceptible to joint problems, such as arthritis, rheumatism, due to the Saturn influence. She may also have sensitive skin at times. A dry climate may require a diet with plenty of oil and protein. With rashes or ''little friends'' she will scratch and chew with all her determination. Grooming should be thorough and frequent.

Capricorn loves to eat and is very practical about it. She is not a gourmet like Libra; gravy and dry food will do just fine.

Your Capricorn dog may tend to have brief spells of depression. Lots of affection and regular exercise will help. She is her own being, and entitled to her moods.

She will be respectful of people because secretly she knows she is one of them. This is what causes some of her problems with jealousy. Fortunately, she has a sense of humor.

As a parent, she may be rather strict and formidable. She will take the responsibility very seriously.

Capricorn may find close relationships difficult at times due to her innate shyness and reserve. Yet, when all is considered, her constant devotion and reliability will bring a sense of security to your home and a dependability to your routine. If you love stability, she is your best friend.

Notes on Your Capricorn Dog

The Puppy _____

_____

_____

_____

_____

Training _____

_____

_____

_____

_____

Public Relations _____

_____

_____

_____

_____

Aquarius

Aquarius

January 21-February 19
Element — Air
Symbol — The Water Bearer
Polarity — Yang, Masculine
Ruling Planet — Uranus/Saturn

One Aquarius pup learned to outwit a six-foot fence by climbing up the inside of a double-sided gate about three feet to where the outside board was missing. He could then jump out and return to his yard by jumping through the broken slat and falling to the bottom. Neighbors reported his daily roaming, but his owner continued to leave him, and always found him in the yard. One day when she returned home unexpectedly early, she met him on the street. The neighbors' tales were true, but she could not understand how her Aquarius had managed to know what time she usually returned from work. She had punished Aquarius for digging out under the fence, so he simply climbed through the gate and returned home before she did.

Aquarius can be fixed in his opinions and is not easily persuaded that he is wrong.

Your puppy will be continually curious, and he loves mystery. Everything will intrigue him. He will appear perceptive and sharper than other signs. He often cocks his head and seems to be pondering great projects.

Aquarius is ruled by Uranus, the planet of extremes, so he is unpredictable and full of contradictions. He will be a surprise from day to day.

Aquarius will love the outdoors. At times he may appear to be in a fog, and occasionally bump into things on his neighborhood strolls.

Gregariousness is a part of the Aquarian makeup. All animals will be his friend, and he loves people. Emotional tension will disturb him as he is very intuitive. Even as a pup he will manage a nonchalant live-and-let-live attitude; and let opinions pass, yours and his.

The Water Bearer sign is idealistic and intelligent, even if he is unconventional.

Aquarius may blissfully do exactly what you want, or what you don't want. Unpredictable? Be prepared for his training.

The Puppy

The Aquarius puppy will be a quivering ball of stubborn, independent electricity.

Aquarius is the New Age puppy. He is everyone's brother. He also needs to be free, and yet has an ability to make you and others revolve around him.

Even as a pup he won't need your support, as Cancer does. He will not be too concerned about what you think of him, and he won't bother to form opinions about you either. As a puppy, he is clever, inventive, and quick to learn; even if he is erratic.

Aquarius needs his personal independence. He will be friendly and loyal, but his individuality is very important to him, and he is used to being different. Conformity gives him no security. Therefore, as Aquarius is kind and friendly, he is also obstinate and may insist on his own way. His manners could be very disconcerting.

Training

As a trainer, be aware that Aquarius has a scientific mind. He'll be very independent and original. He loves the fresh approach and dislikes dull routine.

Your Aquarius may appear to be the absent-minded professor at times. He may have an illusive, dreamy quality. He seems not to pay attention to your commands, and he may or may not recall his lessons. He is learning when he pretends not to be. His inner sensitivity lets him know your desires, and he is also adept at projecting his feelings to you if you are open to communication. A high intellect makes it easy for him to learn if he doesn't hit a rebellious or eccentric streak. He can, in his way, be as tactless as Sagittarius. He can also be set in his ways but with sudden shifts in behavior. Be prepared for anything in his training, but remember that he won't be too concerned with your reactions or opinions.

He may react to your commands by absent-mindedly mulling them over. Then he may do exactly what you don't want. He may also go in several directions at once unless he is trained to follow logical commands. How you will wish that his mental speed could be harnessed.

Aquarius won't need to be the leader in a class as does Leo or Aries. He will not be impressed or pressured by his fellow students. He will love them all in his detached way. Their opinion of him is none of his business.

Aquarius is a real humanitarian, and believes in justice for all. He is a loner and his cool demeanor may make close relationships difficult. He will have a calming effect on his public even if he is not too emotionally involved.

Public Relations

Your Aquarius will present a strange, aloof sophistication to his friends. He is fascinating and dynamic, even if he is not terribly warm and endearing. Aquarius can be a great guide to all as he is sympathetic and helpful, yet he can maintain professional detachment. Because the Aquarian dog is ruled by extremes, it may be very helpful to consult his Moon sign to get an indication which way he will lean. Other signs may tend to temper some of his attitudes.

Aquarian dogs often have a fear of high places. Elevators, outside stairways, and bridges are not their favorite places.

Although he may be forgetful and absent-minded, he can sense your feelings and he is intuitively aware of all his surroundings. He loves crowds and having lots of friends. He is also a natural rebel and won't want his friends to be too intimate. He is a mass of contradictions.

Since Aquarius is the sign of the New Age, your Aquarius will truly work at being everyone's brother, possibly at the expense of isolation from close relationships. He has the ability to be entirely nonjudgmental. He won't boss other pets and is content to figure them out in his own loving way.

Natural curiosity will cause him to inspect everything with the thoroughness of Virgo.

He may be silent at times, but these periods seldom last long. Don't be bothered by his melancholy, it's sometimes hard to be all things to everyone.

All children fascinate Aquarius. As a parent, he won't be affectionate, but he will be extremely interested in his pups' activities.

A female Aquarius will want her pups to be independent and mature. She will be able to handle all their puppy problems in a detached, diplomatic way.

Aquarius will dislike extremes in temperature. Heat may cause him to be depressed and moody and he will want to be alone.

He may have a tendency to have circulation problems. There may also be a weakness of the legs or ankles. Aquarians are prone to accidents, usually due to lack of attention.

Your Aquarius should be encouraged to have as much physical activity as possible to improve his circulation. Plenty of fresh air is a must. Bland food will help his digestion if he is upset.

At the end of the day, an Aquarius is often nervous and tense. A quiet time in the evening may allow him to unwind and it may also improve his sleep.

Your Aquarius's desire is to help and to serve everyone. He will be the one that makes the rounds at your parties and is concerned about your happiness. He may also have some unusual ways of expressing his love of humanity.

He can be your faithful peacemaker in a crisis or your unconventional guide to free-living. The choice is yours because he is here to serve.

Notes on Your Aquarius Dog

The Puppy

_____
_____
_____
_____
_____
_____

Training

_____
_____
_____
_____
_____
_____

Public Relations

_____
_____
_____
_____
_____

Pisces

Pisces

February 20-March 20
Element — Water
Symbol — Two Fish
Polarity — Yin, Feminine
Ruling Planet — Neptune

The Puppy

Your little Pisces pup will be cuddly, soft, and adorable. She could pose for any puppy-chow commercial because of her lovable softness and delightful manner. Her charm is childlike and she is the most holdable little angel you will find.

When she is separated from mom and the kids she will cling to you like a little ball of fluffy fur. She is the most sensitive of all the Sun signs, so be sure to be gentle with voice and actions. Pisces will be aware of your every move and frown.

Your Pisces pet will love a soft, smooth bed. Velour over a downy pillow or soft towels will do fine. She'd probably like to stay close to you, yet away from any disturbing noises on the television.

Pisces is an unworldly little pup, and very impressionable. If there are other dogs in the family, you may find yourself rescuing her and wishing your other pets could be better behaved.

As you begin to try to settle into a schedule with your pet, you may realize that your routine is totally out of her range of response. She may appear a little vague and careless. She's easily confused and indecisive about behavior.

Your little dreamer prefers to eat when she is hungry and play when the spirit moves her. She may sleep all day and wander at night. Any attempt to settle her into a routine will dampen her puppy daydreams and she'll be hurt and depressed.

The Pisces needs a hero, and she has chosen you. She has a strong need to identify; but if you are a domineering Aries, a powerful Scorpio, or a schedule-loving Capricorn, she will have difficulty keeping the pace.

Pisces is romantic and dreamy. She often escapes from reality to a land of fluffy clouds, dog biscuits, soft ferns and fairy tales.

She will love to be helpful, and will follow you from room to room watching your every move. She will glow if you talk to her and include her in your work. Don't be surprised if she wanders off after another pet, or gets lost in a daydream. She is easily distracted. All Pisces pups aspire to be lap dogs, so if your dog is a Saint Bernard or a Great Dane, be prepared for problems.

Her gentle charm and deep compassion for everyone makes her easy to love, and she will need lots of affection. Sensitive intuition will tell her when you feel cross or unhappy. She will try cuddling with you first, and if she is rebuffed she may drift off into her own puppy world.

In all things she will need your attention and encouragement. She is very unsure of herself. Even paper training needs to be gentle and compassionate. Pisces will slip into moody depression if not treated kindly. Now, on to sensitivity training.

Training

Robust dog play is not her style, neither is police dog or military training—unless her breed or Moon sign alter her Pisces nature.

All her sweetness may have won your little Pisces an exalted place in your home, and she may be slightly pampered. Training is a must, even for a princess.

She won't balk or pout at your attempts at training. You will need to be gentle but firm with her evasive behavior and confusion in learning commands. She may be so charming as she perches on your velvet chair that you hesitate to remind her it is off limits.

Training classes may not be for her. Remember she is easily distracted, and will be influenced by other students. She does not like competition—like the Aries pup—and ambition is not her style. Pisces will be timid by nature, but she is talented and a natural mimic. With encouragement, she can become an elegant performer. She may have difficulty conforming to a training pattern. Don't plan your obedience work every afternoon at 4:00 P.M., since she may not be ready. She could be involved in a puppy dream or watching a butterfly.

Once you have her attention, she wants to please you. She will retire when criticized. She's really not enthusiastic about discipline, schedules, or routines, but she will learn because she loves you. Above all, she wants to serve.

She is a humble, compassionate student who will need care and patience. She may not understand why it is important to walk on your left or sit in one position, but she will perform for you in her easy-going style. If she fails a lesson, she will blame herself. Don't try to fool her, her intuitive nature can sense a snow job.

Pisces is the Sun sign of the Twelfth House and, therefore, contains within it traits of the other signs. This will increase her trainability as she will display the enthusiasm of Aries, the devotion of Capricorn, and the sense of fun of Cancer. With her versatility the young Pisces will have plenty of personality and popularity in her relations with her public.

Public Relations

The Pisces pooch will mix well with other pets and people. Few things will excite her to violent action. She can bear all kinds of insults and continue to dream on.

She dislikes boisterous, aggressive play, and her public may be hard on her nerves. She is seldom aroused to fight back, but when she is she can be quite clever. She won't compete for first place in the family pecking order, but she may charm her way into the driver's seat.

Pisces is an intuitive sign. She will know what you are feeling. Because her sign holds aspects of all the twelve signs there may be many of the other Zodiac characteristics behind her humble exterior. Deep wisdom and compassion are her trademark. The combination of Sun sign effects may make her quite a puzzling character, but this will be tempered by breed and heredity.

Pisces health may not be robust. She may not take care of herself, and like Libra will need her rest and privacy.

Your Pisces may have a slow metabolism. She could be slow in getting started in the morning, and a little fuzzy-headed after naps. After hectic activity or heated emotions she will need time to withdraw and meditate. Soft music and peaceful surroundings will calm her nerves.

Pisces pooches may have foot problems and perhaps extraordinarily large or tiny paws. Youngsters often have what is called "puppy paws," and you may find yourself wondering if she will ever grow into those feet.

She may tend to put on weight in her middle years, so you will need to watch her diet. She is not a gourmet like Libra, but she may be so lovable that she may get too many handouts at the table and becomes a little chubby.

Bland food is best for Pisces, and she will prefer certain textures as well as tastes.

Pisces will have lovely, clear eyes and a happy nature. Pisces is the sign that will try to hide her disappointments with a wistful look, and there will be no tantrums or destruction of property.

Some Pisces have a tendency to develop strange phobias. Many of these appear self-induced because you won't remember any related traumas. Remember that you don't have access to her dream world.

One Pisces dog had a phobia about hats and other headgear. If her owner wore a sun hat or scarf, she ducked under the bed and no amount of coaxing could bring her out. When hats were placed on the floor for her to sniff and investigate, she avoided them and left the room. No one could remember any problem Pisces ever had with anyone wearing a hat, but the Pisces knew hats were a danger to her.

If you live in an artfully decorated home, Pisces will fit right in. She loves harmony in her surroundings but, ironically, she herself may be a little sloppy or untidy at times. Her own area may be chaos and clutter. She lacks the direction and discipline to have a cleaning schedule.

A female Pisces may need sex counseling and a chaperon. She is such a charmer she will be the most popular gal on the block. She is so impressionable and indecisive about the opposite sex. She hates to hurt anyone's feelings. You will need to lock her in the house at special times, and be the one who says "no" to a suitor's advances. Her child-like nature could make her easy prey for the Scorpio male next door.

As a parent she may be over-indulgent, and she will have difficulty with discipline and control.

Pisces may be sensual, but they are born mystics. One Pisces male I have visited since a pup has the air of a Tibetan llama. He radiates wisdom and compassion, and his deep-dark eyes glitter with love and understanding. He has a way of tilting his head in deep contemplation. This Pisces lives with four cats and maintains an aura of enchanted serenity plus a hint of humor.

Your Pisces will be the most compassionate of all the signs. Your pains and joys will be hers, even if she does try to hide her feelings by walking away for a while to control herself. Her emotions are deep and strong. You will never be without a concerned friend.

She may be able to teach you to be free and unscheduled if you don't have a demanding routine or Sun sign. She will teach you about love, devotion, and daydreams.

Notes on Your Pisces Dog

The Puppy _____
_____
_____
_____
_____
_____

Training _____
_____
_____
_____
_____
_____

Public Relations _____
_____
_____
_____
_____

The Moon Signs

Moon Signs

Moon signs involve the position of the Moon at your pet's birth. Moon signs change on the average of every two-and-a-half days. Knowing the Moon sign can give you a greater insight to your dog's character.

Although most people are aware of Sun signs, few consider the effects of the Moon signs, unless they have a birthchart or a friend in astrology. Moon signs, as well as ascendants—the sign of the First House, which rules temperament—are among the reasons that there are such striking differences among members on the same Sun sign.

The less obvious clue to your pet's true nature may be his or her Moon sign. The Sun sign will represent what your pet appears to be, but a Moon sign may reveal his or her hidden emotional climate and motivation. As your pet matures, he or she may reveal more of the Moon sign tendencies.

You may find it worthwhile to consult an ephemeris or an astrologer to discover your pet's Moon sign. Again, you will need the hour of birth, because Moon signs, like Sun signs, do not change at midnight.

Owners who know the date of birth of their pets may find their pet's birthday is in the middle of a Moon sign and not need to know the hour of a particular day.

If the hour is needed, and is not available, you may need to study both the Moon signs involved that appear in that one day.

Owners with pets who have unknown birthdays may skim through all the Moon signs and make an intuitive estimate of their dog's character and corresponding sign.

Remember that if you are reasonably sure of your pet's Sun sign (you know an approximate date of birth), the Moon sign may be the sign that contains the characteristics that were not found in your pet's Sun sign. Your dog is a combination of both signs.

Now, let's move on to a more intimate investigation of the Moon signs and what makes your dog pant or bark.

* The pronoun he or she will follow the polarity of the Moon sign in the same manner that it was used with Sun signs.

Moon in Aries

Emotional Nature

The Moon in Aries has a different effect than the Sun in Aries, because the Moon is a water influence. In a fire sign, the Moon may create steam, or in your pet's case, an abundance of enthusiasm which expresses itself in a very yappy manner. Your Arian Moon pet may throw off an abundance of energy, and "Me First" is his middle name.

He has a quick, changeable mind and emotions. At his worst, he may seem pushy and selfishly assertive. You can buffer his impetuous nature by helping him develop patience through good training habits, and love.

He may have a tendency to be quick-tempered and his reactions are just as rapid. The Aries Moon pet appears to be sure of himself.

Be careful that his wounded pride and fast reactions don't result in a snarl or nip which both of you—or perhaps your neighbor—will live to regret. Although the Aries' temper is quick it is soon over. Unfortunately, the damage already done may be severe.

The Aries Moon pet's emotional need for freedom and independence will dominate his view of the world.

The Moon in Aries World

The Aries Moon pet has extremely sharp senses which may cause him to react quickly without much thought or planning. He may appear high-strung with a hot temper due to nervous strain. His nerves, and yours, can be calmed by removing unnecessary excitement or stimulation from his environment.

The Aries dog needs to have one master, or at least not an entire household of people making demands on his rapid-fire senses.

The Moon in Aries dog has enthusiasm and drive that will move him from one project to another. He may never complete anything, which in some cases may be a blessing—he didn't chew all the way through the strap of your new shoes.

He has so much energy he will be involved in big plans, but with very little attention to detail. When his plans fall apart, due to lack of attention, he will have equal enthusiasm for his next project.

If training and discipline are to be part of his world, you will need to take a firm hand and leash. Although he may resist your authority at first, your Aries Moon loves an audience and will carry through with obedience for your approval.

Your Aries Moon pooch can't stay angry for long, and he is usually the impulsive life of the party.

Personal Relations

The Aries theme song is "I Did It My Way." He will love to forge a new path, and may resent your advice.

You may be wondering how to relate to this Moon sign. He will adore you if you present him with new experiences—not the same old fetch-the-stick routine. Also, involve him with new friends by taking him for a walk on a different block. He loves novelty and can create his own excitement.

Because the Aries Moon dog is headstrong and jumps to conclusions quickly, he may have bouts of depression or anger. This will not last long. His enthusiasm will return quickly.

He is not domestic but he needs to feel important at home. If he does not feel valued, he may resort to sexual conquests outside the home. Beware Libra and Pisces pooches.

An Aries Moon pet will keep you jumping. If you want a challenge, he'll be there for you.

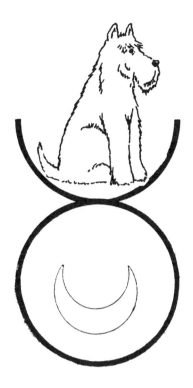

Moon in Taurus

Emotional Nature

When the Moon is in Taurus, its restless ways are steadied. Your Taurus Moon pet will be conservative and capable of deep concentration.

Taurus is the most stable emotional sign of the Moon. Your pet will be persistent, positive in nature, determined in projects, and optimistic of heart. She may also tend to be ambitious, and you may need to guide this ambition—obedience training classes rather than digging up the flower beds.

The Moon in Taurus may cause a somewhat obstinate nature, but your Taurus will also be self-reliant and practical. She can be self-indulgent and you may need to broaden her interests. She will benefit from your attention and invention of new games such as chase-the-tennis ball. On occasion she may need to be drawn out of her conservative shell.

She will always be practical, because her head rules her heart. She may appear a little hard-headed in training, (see Sun Signs—Taurus—Training), but she has a good deal of common sense, and can be counted on in emergencies.

The Moon in Taurus World

The Taurus Moon pet may react slowly to the events in her world, but she responds fully, and once her mind is made up she can be stubborn. When presented with some new event, like a strange toy or new food, there will be no upsets or quick decisions like Aries. She will study the new material, and decide her response slowly and carefully. The Moon's influence becomes very practical and stable in Taurus, not impulsive.

A Taurus will love to gather resources—like old bones, or rawhide chews—and conserve these for a rainy day. She can be practical to the point of exasperation.

Your pet will love good grooming habits and also have nice manners. She may appear a little old fashioned. All of these attributes will help her in her personal relations.

Personal Relations

The Taurus Moon pet will love you and your family. She will need family support and also love family traditions, such as after dinner walks, or morning coffee and cuddling.

She may tend toward possessiveness, but on the whole, she will be sociable and love fun and games.

Taurus can be a sensual pooch, and she appreciates all the benefits of a solid relationship, such as scratches behind the ears, and table scraps.

She has a highly developed sense of taste and touch, and relishes overtures of food and petting.

A Moon in Taurus pet prefers relationships with owners who are devoted, domestic, and faithful. Just like she is.

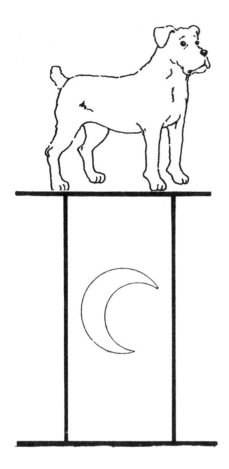

Moon in Gemini

Emotional Nature

When the Moon is in Gemini it becomes unstable. This may cause the emotional nature of your pet to be somewhat nervous. The Moon will stimulate the imagination and creativity, but may also cause your Gemini to forget his training and manners at times.

The positive aspects of the Moon in Gemini are intelligence and inventiveness, while the negative aspects involve a frivolous and fickle nature.

Like a true example of the sign of the Twins, the Moon in your Gemini's emotions may swing back and forth rapidly between positive and negative. This dualistic emotional nature will make the Moon in Gemini very versatile and lively, but also moody. This emotional instability can be influenced by other signs, so check his Sun signs and hope for a stabilizing earth sign like Taurus.

If he is indecisive, changeable, and restless, physical and mental activity will help him calm and balance his emotions. When you see him start to pace around the house going from room to room, or start to scratch himself all over, a good long run or perhaps some training-time will help to center and direct his energies.

All the Gemini Moon's quick physical and mental energy will often make him seem fearless. Perhaps he just doesn't think before he jumps that six foot fence. What was on the other side did not concern him until he got there.

He will bounce back from defeats or depressions easily. He has an optimistic nature. His youthful attitudes tend to keep him acting young, and he will view his adult world with the eyes of a puppy.

The Moon in Gemini World

The Moon in Gemini pet quickly senses events in his world, but his judgments may be poor or he may change his mind often. He may dart swiftly after a ball, stumble over a rock, and then wander off to sniff a tree. He will look up at you quizzically as you repeat, "Bring me the ball."

The Gemini loves scientific experiments and observation. He may watch an ant on the road with intensity, but then he may be distracted and step on it.

He will usually need to do more than one thing at a time. New experiences are a must because boredom is very painful for a Gemini. His mind must be active, and if you can direct it toward education and training, you will have a willing pupil.

The Gemini Moon pet will love travel, variety, and breaks in routine. He will love to see more of his world, and usually enjoys riding in cars, boats, or even bicycle baskets.

Personal Relations

The Moon in Gemini pet will benefit from your practical leadership. He will not resent your being the boss as long as he has some freedom.

With all his nervous tension he will need your help in developing perseverance and deliberation. Just don't be too demanding or routine about your relationship. He'll need the freedom of time on his own to play, or to study a bug.

Because of his dual nature, the Gemini Moon pet can handle crowds. He can have several masters in one household. With his charm and easy ways he'll make every one feel important.

He may be a little vain, and you may catch him prancing and watching his reflection in a window.

A Gemini Moon pet will be a good teacher. If you want a versatile life-style like his, follow his lead.

nature may be a plus if she has to endure boisterous children or a house full of cats, but you may find yourself coaxing her to get out into the world and live a little.

The Gemini Moon pet will not be passive about her possessions. What's hers is hers, and she can be obsessive about it. She will like to look out on the world from inside her home, so she can keep an eye on her belongings.

The Moon in Cancer World

Due to her emotional sensitivity, the Cancer Moon pet will be well aware of what is going on in her world, but she may not show it. She has a tendency to remain serene and think about things, rather than to react.

She has a good memory. The Cancer Moon dog will not search for new experiences, but she does remember, absorb, and record what happens in her life. She will recall all past details and recognize old friends. This is the sign that will remember someone you briefly met five years ago. As she stands by, wagging her tail, you will frantically search your mind for a name. It's too bad she can't speak or she would tell you.

The Moon in Cancer needs a creative outlet. With her powerful emotions and tendency toward brooding, she should be kept busy.

She dislikes physical work and would rather stay in or near home, so her activities may be somewhat limited. A job around home and family, like following the kids, will improve her self-image and make her more fun to be with.

Personal Relations

A Moon in Cancer pet will demand your time and attention in her own way. If she is affectionate and loving toward you and your family, she will expect her favors to be returned. If they are not, she will sulk. She has an uncanny way of making people try to please her by causing them to feel guilty. She can be a real martyr if things do not go her way. She will pout to break your heart, but at least she won't have temper tantrums.

Cancer is the pooch whose sad-eyed looks, when you pick up the car keys, can cause you to stay around a while and scratch her stomach.

The Cancer Moon needs to cherish and protect all her relationships. She has the family instinct and will be very possessive about you, your family, or her puppies.

She will need your help in learning not to be too dependent.

She will always be sensitive to the feelings of others. If you want domestic loyalty that can't be matched, she's your choice.

Moon in Cancer

Emotional Nature

The Moon is most at home in the sign of Capricorn. Your Moon in Cancer pet will have her emotional highs and lows. Because her emotional nature is so open and sensitive, she will need a great deal of peace and quiet. She will require her privacy and place to contemplate her life.

The Cancer Moon pet will not like to be rushed or hindered in her daily tasks.

This sign is very domestic. She will not like to leave home and travel like the Gemini Moon pet. She loves the domestic life.

Unless her Sun sign or other aspects show activity and force, she may tend to be too passive. Her passive

His generous, positive, confident nature is usually matched by physical strength and vitality. Your Leo Moon pet can be a real dynamo. His gay, affectionate nature will make him a popular leader in his world.

The Moon in Leo World

The Moon in Leo pet loves luxury. A life of sophisticated pleasure is his ideal. He has a need to appear grand, dashing, and immensely popular. This is the pet that would love to be a movie star. He'd revel in the flashing lights, huge crowds, and elegant attention. If possible, your pet might love to do commercials. He would look charming stepping off a yacht and advertising the most expensive dog collar available.

The Leo Moon pooch may be extremely concerned with status. He may see his world as a social ladder at times. You will need to watch him for snobbish behavior. If this gets out of hand it may interfere with his need to have lots of friends.

Personal Relations

Forming a relationship with your Leo Moon pet may be a challenge.

A male Leo Moon pet will put you on a pedestal, and if you keep up your end of the relationship, he will idolize you forever. Your male Leo Moon pet may be a little conceited himself and you may find he has his own pedestal, right next to yours.

A female Leo Moon pet will feel the same way about your pedestal, but she won't have one of her own. She will be more balanced and modest. If your relationship has some lows, she will be very crushed and blame herself for any failures.

Whether male or female, the Leo Moon pet may need some help in avoiding an over-bearing, if not conceited nature. He does have his good points. He is very loyal and responsible in the home. He is a good leader, vigorous and optimistic.

With his self-reliance and love of freedom, the Leo Moon dog usually needs a mission. With luck you can help him pick something constructive.

The Leo must be interested in something before he can learn. Appeal to his heart first, and hopefully his head will follow his heart. Once he is emotionally involved, he will relate easily and learn quickly.

Although the Leo Moon may be a little egotistical and may fail to consider the feelings of others, he loves relationships, especially if they expand his world.

He is a good organizer, but he may get a bit bossy.

If you want a pet with a royal nature, then a Leo Moon is your king.

Moon in Leo

Emotional Nature

Your Moon in Leo pet is a born leader, with the vigor and self-reliance that fit his symbol, the Lion.

When the Moon is in this fire sign, your pet will be very loveable and loving. He will tend to be very idealistic about life, and he needs to wisely choose his friends and projects. When he does make a poor choice of plans, or friends disappoint him, he can become very bitter.

The Leo Moon's firmness in sticking to decisions can be a fine attribute at times, especially on the training field. When firm determination turns to stubbornness, it can be a problem. This is the sign that may refuse to see the writing on the wall. In a noble attempt to keep the faith he may hold to his convictions long after they have been proven wrong.

Your Virgo Moon pet may appear a little critical, especially if there are younger pets in the home or if her world goes off schedule.

The Moon in Virgo World

The Virgo Moon pet reacts to her world by analyzing everything in her meticulous way. She can be very discriminating to the point of being overly critical at times.

She is practical and down to earth, and she sees life as it is. Whatever she learns, she will try to apply in some way.

A Virgo Moon pet will be interested in her diet and health. With her tendency to worry, she'll be concerned about what she eats.

This sign usually shows a green thumb, or paw, and she may be very interested in digging, especially around plants. Remember, this is an earth sign, and her meticulous nature may require some investigation into the ground.

A Moon in Virgo pet will have a good sense of order. Her lack of confidence in her abilities may cause her to be a bit fussy about her world. She is the sign who will be a good observer of the neighborhood dogs. She will carefully note all their activities, safe in her role as a recorder, not a leader.

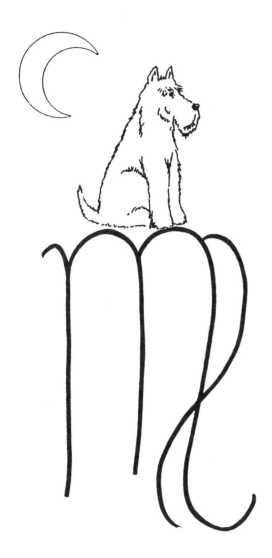

Moon in Virgo

Emotional Nature

The Moon tends to soften the exacting Virgo nature. Your Moon in Virgo pet may seem a little timid or have a slightly nervous disposition. She may tend to worry about small things, and large upsets may affect her digestion.

The Moon in Virgo dog will have a practical mind and a good memory. She will be shrewd when bargaining for favors or tasty tidbits. She can also be very logical and dedicated, but be careful that she doesn't get too entangled in details. This is the sign that can do well in obedience training if she doesn't get caught up in nit-picking or fear of failure. (See Sun Signs—Virgo—Training.)

Personal Relations

If you are a physical fitness buff, your Virgo Moon pet will be right beside you. She loves to work out and is a great admirer of good health.

The Virgo Moon dog also likes a healthy mind, so you may find you need to keep up with her training. She will love a review now and then just to be sure she knows all the commands down to the last detail.

A Moon in Virgo dog will be interested in the community. It will please her greatly if you show the same interest when you go on walks together.

She will be a very stable partner, and may tend to suffer in silence if the relationship isn't what she wished. Most Virgo Moon pets will struggle to keep a relationship working. They may become overly conscientious and calculate their every move.

If she knows she is loved, your Virgo Moon pet will relax her hold on minute details. When you are both well-organized and efficient, she will be a proud pooch.

collection of *objects d'art*. His tastes may not be like yours, but he will have his own sense of beauty—a bent plastic pen, with tooth holes in expressive places, or a brightly decorated piece of wrapping paper.

Although he may be self-indulgent at times, the Libra Moon will be fun to live with, since he will try to keep his world in perfect balance.

The Moon in Libra World

The Libra Moon pet will love to share in all the good things of life. This will include all your special snacks. He'll also enjoy romantic walks in the moonlight, and for him, three is not a crowd.

He will know all the right people and the right places. The Libra charm will make him a success in high places, and he will usually arrive at the meat market just when the butcher is wondering what to do with some scraps. (He has already met the butcher, won him over, and learned his schedule.)

Your Libra Moon pet will view his world through very accurate senses. He will occasionally need to judge events or people, but his primary concern is to keep things balanced. He will find decisions hard to make, but a good relationship with you can temper his indecisiveness.

Personal Relations

The Libra Moon pooch really wants to please you. He enjoys working on a partnership. With his friendly, easy-going charm he will have lots of friends, but he needs a devoted master to help him with his problems of indecision and lack of self-reliance.

He does have a real need for good companionship, because sometimes he can be too independent or capricious.

The female Libra Moon pet will do best with a strong partner. She will be rather aloof and refined at times. She will dislike coarseness in any form. This is the Moon sign that would enjoy bows in her hair after grooming and would be the last one to paw them out.

With the Libra Moon's excellent manners you can always depend on him to do the right thing. He will also expect good manners from you in return, and he will be offended if you are rude. If you step on his paw by mistake, please apologize politely.

Your Libra Moon pet has his charm, and he knows how to use it. If you are planning an elegant dinner gathering, be sure to include him. He'll be the hit of the party.

Moon in Libra

Emotional Nature

Your Libra Moon pet will be a study in courtesy, charm, and diplomacy. He could be mistaken for a member of the diplomatic corps as he wanders among his associates smoothing ruffled fur and offering friendship.

He may appear a little ambitious, but he is gentle and affectionate as well.

The Moon in Libra pet loves beauty. He will display good taste in color and form. Be sure his private area is well-decorated with a good sense of design and beauty.

This is the Moon sign that may be a collector of art. You may need to check his special hiding places for his

The Scorpio will search for new challenges. She is always ready for play and is determined to dominate every situation.

Pride can be a bit of a problem for the Scorpio Moon pet, and you may need to stand your ground to stay in her world.

The Moon in Scorpio World

The Scorpio Moon pet has a good sense of perception and her powers of observation are sharp and accurate. She can spot a cat hidden by a bush at fifty paces. Her judgment is shrewd, and she has the way of a scientist when looking at her world.

A Moon in Scorpio dog will need to learn to see her environment with an optimistic view. With her excellent memory, she has a tendency to hold on to unhappy memories which tend to effect her present situation.

She has excellent will-power and determination in facing any problem. Once she has a goal, she will not stop until she completes her task. This could include secret investigations into your library. You may return home some day and find every book on the floor, and a few covers chewed.

The Moon in Scorpio yields a very strong sexual nature, and also a need for secrecy. She may yearn for secret, romantic meetings, and you may end up with a few surprises. If male, your Scorpio may disappear for periods of time and return in an extremely nonchalant manner.

This need for secrecy may also affect the Scorpio Moon's personal relations.

Personal Relations

Relationships won't always be easy for the Moon in Scorpio pet, but with her persistence she can overcome many challenges. She has high ideals, initiative, ambition, and the courage of her convictions. With all this in her favor she will usually end up in control of her relationships. You will need to cultivate the same qualities to win her loyalty.

Female Scorpio Moon pets tend to be jealous, so beware of your behavior toward other pets in her presence. Because of her secretive nature, you will not see her disapproval, but she may have an eye toward revenge. She could just sneak off and eat the other dog's dinner, or bury his toys.

Your passionate, emotional Scorpio Moon will love sensual pleasures. You can win her affections with a good steak bone or a gentle massage of her furry head.

In spite of her need for secrecy, the Scorpio Moon pet will be very loyal and a good sign to have on your side on any occasion.

Moon in Scorpio

Emotional Nature

The Moon in this water sign gives a highly emotional nature. Your Moon in Scorpio pet will be emotionally intense, and have a great deal of animal magnetism. She will be very sensitive.

At times she will appear introverted, but this will be to cover her inner tension which she finds difficult to deal with. She may sink into deep, restrained moodiness as she handles inner turmoil.

A Moon in Scorpio pet will need to work and play hard to let off steam.

The Scorpio Moon can be tactless and irritable if crossed. Her possessive nature and emotional intensity may cause her to be manipulative.

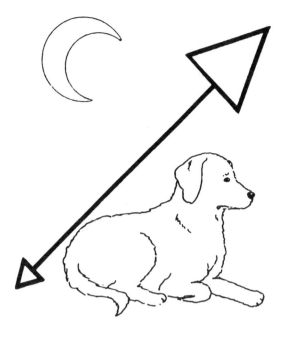

A female Moon in Sagittarius will be sensitive and shy in her refined way. She may wait to be spoken to first, but then she can really chatter. Both sexes are known for their almost careless enthusiasm for meeting and greeting everyone in their world.

The Moon in Sagittarius World

With all this zest for life, your pet will require lots of exercise. Because he'll love sports, it shouldn't be hard to satisfy the need. He is convinced that he is lucky. The Sagittarius Moon will be so eager to make progress in all his activities that he may over estimate his own strengths and talents. He has the ability to think quickly, but not for long periods of time. Discussions will need to be brief.

The Moon in Sagittarius pet's senses are very sharp and accurate. He is intelligent and will see his world very clearly. He will usually show good judgment, and take all issues into consideration.

In your home he will be aware of everything that is happening at once, and may fly from one person to another in a blur of fur. He'll just have to be a part of everything at once.

His exuberance can be a problem or a plus. When he starts crazy projects you may be able to disengage him by going for a walk. Outdoors is more fun than tearing up magazines or trying to play with the cat.

Wherever your Sagittarius Moon dog is, he always walks like he knows where he is going—and perhaps you'd like to go with him. You can both decide en route where you are going.

Moon in Sagittarius

Emotional Nature

The Moon in Sagittarius gives a rather restless and cheerful nature. Your fire sign Moon pet will be independent and also a frequent talker. His moves, like his bark, will be urgent and quick.

The Moon in Sagittarius will have intuitive powers. This is the dog that will run to the phone before it rings, and sense your every mood. His second sight can be an inspiration.

He will love the outdoors and also love to travel. With all that energy and jovial nature he can be lots of fun on any trip. His optimistic and outspoken nature will cause him to stop along the way to chat, even if others don't feel as friendly.

Personal Relations

The Sagittarius Moon pet loves his personal freedom. If he must be confined for long periods, watch out for a small revolution.

He loves to combine business with pleasure, so, as he heels at your side, he may sneak in a sniff at a tree.

A Moon in Sagittarius will need to learn to curb his carelessness and bluntness.

He makes a great companion, although he may expect you to follow his lead. You can work this out during an obedience class. He'll love any social gathering.

Moon in Sagittarius pets hate failure in a relationship. He will leave the scene quickly if it looks like he is going to be scolded or punished. He will return when the air is cleared with his usual bouncy optimism. He'll prance and bring you his ball. "Want to play?" How can you refuse?

Capricorn Moon's are very responsible and persistent in all their actions and duties. She may take life so seriously that she becomes a workhorse and forgets about the joy of just napping in the sun or chasing a bee.

Your Capricorn Moon pet will have a mood of stoic acceptance to whatever happens. She is a born realist. As she matures you will need to be sure she remembers how to play and how to look at the light side of her world.

The Moon in Capricorn World

The Capricorn Moon pet will respond quickly, but it may take a while for things to soak into her senses. She will be alert and eager to learn, but her initial reactions may be a little wary, or hostile. At times her reactions may seem cool, and she could be a loner in her own self-sufficient way.

A Capricorn Moon would benefit from a boisterous, loving family, or at least the presence of other pets.

This sign will often search for some position of power in the home, and feel badly if she does not attain some degree of authority. She can be ambitious and self-important at times.

This may be a difficult Moon sign for a female. She may become a bit of a martyr in her own home, and not have the fire or pluck to state her own case in relationships.

Personal Relations

In relationships, the Capricorn Moon pet will tend to put all her eggs in one basket. She can become obsessed with one person, and if things don't go her way, she will become depressed.

You can perk her up from her gloom with lots of attention and love.

She has a very practical nature, and likes a dependable routine in her life.

Her sense of duty is resolute, and she may be so busy with obligations she forgets to have fun. If she's been guarding your yard or garage all day, go out and toss a few sticks for her. She'll benefit by the distraction, and it will ease her nerves. You might like it too.

If you take the time to involve her in warm, fun-filled relationships, she will prove to be a loving companion.

Moon in Capricorn

Emotional Nature

The Moon's usual sensitizing influence is diminished by Capricorn's somber nature. Your Capricorn Moon pooch will be reserved, cautious, and prudent. Her practical, common-sense can be a blessing, but she will tend to be gloomy and cool at times.

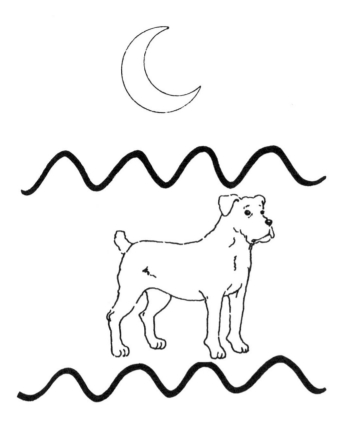

The Aquarian Moon's need for independence and his unconventional nature may cause him to lead a lonely life. All his originality and unpredictability makes him a popular pooch in the neighborhood, but he may fail to develop close emotional relationships.

The Moon in Aquarius pet loves lots of change and variety in his life. He may also be prone to anxiety and tension if he has so many things going at once that he becomes over-stimulated. Sometimes being a social director can be too much.

The Aquarian Moon male is very broad-minded and a "free thinker." The female will be intellectual, and she might have ideas about the New Age feminine movement. Both sexes will have an open and accepting view of the world.

The Moon in Aquarius World

The Aquarius Moon pet accurately senses his world. His reactions will be clear and steady. He'll also have a good balance between heart and head. He can be rational and still be emotional.

The lunar Aquarian can set the guidelines for the new canine society. He will investigate all new trends that involve freedom. Often seeking his own freedom, he will blaze a trail for others. This may be the dog that can slip the latch on the gate and get the other pets to follow him out.

A Moon in Aquarius pet loves to shock people. Nothing is taboo to this pooch. He will scratch whatever itches regardless of where he is or who is there.

The Moon in Aquarius dog will have good intentions, but he may not always have wisdom or use good judgment. With his wide range of interests, he'll need lots of friends and relationships to satisfy his many-sided character.

Personal Relations

The Moon in Aquarius pet needs his freedom, but he may not be too concerned about you having yours. All things considered, he will be a good companion; witty, easygoing, intelligent and forgiving.

He has the ability to attract people and pets, so you may often find yourself in a crowd.

The Aquarius Moon pet may seem to be too impersonal. At times he may lack warmth and responsiveness. Remember, he is doing his democratic best to please and to lead society, and it is a big job for one pooch. He'll need a practical partner who will understand his position as a model New Age pet.

Moon in Aquarius

Emotional Nature

The Aquarius Moon pet will be a friendly, easy-going dog. He will be sympathetic and understanding while keeping his detached attitude.

This Moon sign will have the innate ability to observe and analyze the moods and actions of others. He may appear aloof, because he usually avoids close involvement so that he can remain impartial.

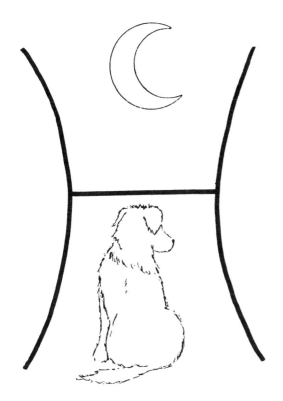

Moon in Pisces

Emotional Nature

The influences of the Moon give your Pisces a variable and often moody emotional nature. She will be highly receptive to your emotions and to those of others around her. She functions like an emotion radar detector, but she has difficulty in knowing what to do with all that input.

The Pisces' moods will change rapidly, but her outward emotional tone appears kind, gentle, and somewhat delicate.

She often suffers from feelings of inferiority.

Your Pisces Moon pet will need to be protected from emotional cruelty. This is definitely not the pet to be left alone with your delinquent youngsters, who may delight in binding her ears over her head or pulling her tail. They may only be playing, but she will feel hurt and rejected.

The male Pisces Moon pet will be very idealistic. Both male and female will be ultra-sensitive, emotional, and

confused by your attempts at logic. You may need to enter the Pisces Moon world to understand your pet.

The Moon in Pisces World

The Pisces Moon pet looks at her world with rose-colored glasses. She is a dreamer, a mystic, and expects the best in all things. She wants to believe that the world is good and beautiful. The manner in which her senses perceive the world may create illusions rather than reality.

She will have a vivid imagination, and she will need your help in developing a realistic outlook on life. This is the pet that will need to realize that each time you go to the pantry it will not always be for dog biscuits.

The Piscean Moon dog will be easily discouraged, and may, in turn, become self-indulgent. If she does not understand her world, she may reject it. If you can help her face reality, she can be very creative.

Remember, a world of strict rules and rigorous training can send a Pisces pooch retreating into her daydreams.

Your Pisces Moon pet will not be critical of you. Her opinions and relationships are based on a delicate combination of fantasy and gentle breezes.

Personal Relations

Your intuitive, sensitive Pisces must follow her intuition. She may be the pet that knows who is coming to dinner before he arrives. Her intuition will increase as she matures.

She has a deep need to do good and help others, often with a little reward. This attitude may cause her to be taken advantage of, especially by more earthy signs. If your Pisces Moon pooch seems to be taken advantage of by the other dogs in the home or neighborhood, check their Sun signs.

In relationships, the Pisces will benefit from an owner or friend with a positive—not apathetic—nature.

She will be a romantic and prone to giving more affection than she receives. She has a very dedicated love nature, even if the love is not returned. You may need to remind yourself that she is not an endless fountain of affection, and return her attentions, because she will be unable to ask for love.

In your relationship with a Moon in Pisces pet, you will be the winner, the more she is loved, the more she will return love.

She may be a little nosey about your friends, but this is just loving concern.

Remember to avoid long projects or training because Pisces does need time to dream. She may have an appointment with the Dog Fairy.

Notes on Your Dog's Moon Sign

Emotional Nature _____

_____

_____

_____

_____

_____

_____

_____

_____

Your Dog's World _____

_____

_____

_____

_____

_____

_____

_____

_____

_____

Notes on Your Dog's Moon Sign

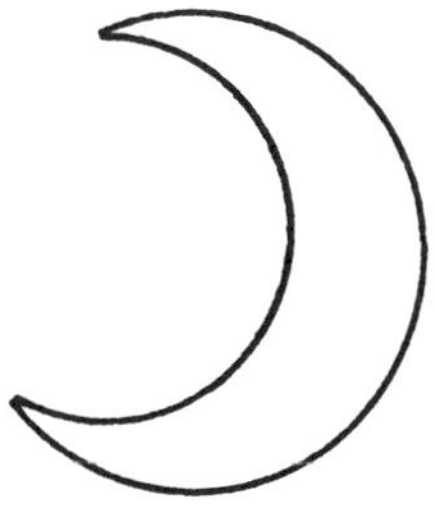

Personal Relations _____

_____
_____
_____
_____
_____

_____
_____
_____
_____
_____
_____
_____

Conclusion

The relationship between the Sun and the Moon is very relevant to the behavior of your dog. If both signs are same, your pet may be rather delicate, and there will be a double dose of the traits of the sign involved. If the Sun and the Moon are in opposite signs: Aries and Libra, Scorpio and Taurus, Gemini and Sagittarius, Cancer and Capricorn, Leo and Aquarius, or Virgo and Pisces, your pet may be unusually tense and very active.

A complete horoscope of your pet will take into consideration the Sun and Moon signs, the ascendant and the eight planets. This will give you a more detailed picture of your pet, and will also explain why dogs born in the same sign can be so different.

To understand your pet's astrology, it will be helpful to relate, or blend, the influences of the Sun and Moon signs. These two influences will accentuate some traits and cause other traits to be blended or tempered. Also, be sure to consider the dog's breed, home environment (other pets and family members), and your own personality or Sun and Moon signs. Your pet will be relating to all of these elements in his or her life, and may draw on, or be influenced by, different aspects of his or her chart in various situations.

From my own experience, I have found that knowing my own pet's Sun and Moon signs has helped greatly in our relationship. During professional training classes I was disturbed by some aspects of my pet's behavior, but after researching the character of Libra, I discovered that my dog was simply being himself.

Further research on other dogs' Sun signs, and the reports by their owners, revealed that most dogs represent their signs in their own individual manner.

Remember, your dog will be expressing his or her astrological makeup in his or her unique way. The Sun and Moon will shed some light to help us understand canine behavior, but some days your dog may seem to be making his or her own little universe.

If you would like to have information about an individualized astrological profile cast for your favorite canine, write to:

Linda L. Lacy
761 Windham Drive
Claremont, CA 91711

Be sure to include your name, address and zip code on a self addressed envelope.